PETER WAITZMAN

Rethink Money

Why Common Money Rules Are Holding You Back

First published by Expedition Money Press 2024

Copyright © 2024 by Peter Waitzman

All rights reserved. No part of this publication may be reproduced, stored or transmitted in any form or by any means, electronic, mechanical, photocopying, recording, scanning, or otherwise without written permission from the publisher. It is illegal to copy this book, post it to a website, or distribute it by any other means without permission.

Peter Waitzman asserts the moral right to be identified as the author of this work.

Peter Waitzman has no responsibility for the persistence or accuracy of URLs for external or third-party Internet Websites referred to in this publication and does not guarantee that any content on such Websites is, or will remain, accurate or appropriate.

Designations used by companies to distinguish their products are often claimed as trademarks. All brand names and product names used in this book and on its cover are trade names, service marks, trademarks and registered trademarks of their respective owners. The publishers and the book are not associated with any product or vendor mentioned in this book. None of the companies referenced within the book have endorsed the book.

First edition

This book was professionally typeset on Reedsy.
Find out more at reedsy.com

For Kevin Jarhung Wu (1977-2013), my Northwestern University roommate & friend who left this world too soon. Kevin was the epitome of brilliance - the smartest person I knew, with an unparalleled depth of knowledge across countless subjects. More than just intelligent, he was an innovative thinker, applying his wisdom in groundbreaking ways. Kevin embodied the art of critical thinking and "zig-zag" problem-solving. This book is dedicated to him & his enduring spirit of intellectual curiosity.

Contents

Preface   iv

I   The Awakening

1   It's Not My Fault   3
2   The Rules We Never Question   7
3   Money Can Buy Happiness   11

II   Education

4   Don't Go To College   19

III   Career

5   Get A Job With A Pension   25
6   Switch Jobs Frequently   29
7   Only Rent An Apartment   33
8   Never Work Just One Job   36

IV   Spending

9   Buy That Gourmet Coffee   43
10   Increase Your Spending   47
11   Play The Lottery   51
12   Make That Impulse Purchase   55
13   Don't Go Grocery Shopping   59

| 14 | Never Buy A $3,000 Car | 63 |
| 15 | Lease A Car | 67 |

V Saving

16	Don't Save For Emergencies	73
17	Only Save $2,500 For Emergencies	77
18	Don't Save In A Savings Account	81
19	Don't Save For College	85
20	Don't Set Financial Goals	90

VI Credit

21	There Is No Good Or Bad Debt	97
22	Get As Much Credit As You Can	101
23	Always Use A Credit Card	105
24	Ignore Your Credit Score	109

VII Family

25	Never Merge Your Finances	115
26	Have Kids Before You Can Afford Them	120
27	Don't Put Money In Your Kid's Name	124

VIII Investing

28	Be An Early Adopter	131
29	Buy Cryptocurrencies	136
30	Don't Worry About Risk Tolerance	141
31	Don't Use An Index Fund	145
32	Ignore Investment Expenses	149
33	Don't Invest Only In What You Know	153
34	Don't Be A Contrarian Investor	157

35	Don't Diversify Your Portfolio	161
36	Don't Rebalance Your Portfolio	165
37	Ignore Capital Gains and Taxes	170

IX   Real Estate

38	Live With Your Parents	177
39	Don't Buy A House	180
40	Always Get The Extended Warranty	184

X   Retirement

41	Ignore Account Contribution Limits	191
42	Don't Save In Retirement Accounts	195
43	Don't Use The Stock Market For Retirement Income	200
44	Have A Mortgage In Retirement	204
45	Don't Retire In America	208
46	End With Nothing	214

XI   Eyes Wide Open

| 47 | The Truth They Don't Want You to Know | 221 |

About the Author   229
Also by Peter Waitzman   230

Preface

So, let's take a ride through the world of personal finance, leaving no stone unturned and no sacred cow un-tipped.

Before we dive in, let me lay my cards on the table. I've been in the trenches of finance for quite some time. I have a degree in economics, worked as an analyst at one of the world's largest banks, and served as an investment and financial advisor, holding Series 7, 66, and insurance licenses. I've helped build several corporate financial wellness programs and earned some alphabet soup along the way - Certified Personal Finance Counselor®, Certified Fund Specialist®, and Accredited Financial Counselor®. Oh, and I'm one hell of a model American (okay, that last one's an exaggeration).

But here's the thing: I'm not sharing this to impress you. If it helps you wade into this book, great. But please understand that I'm not some all-knowing financial deity. I'm still learning, still getting surprised by new information that isn't exactly broadcast on the 6 o'clock news.

Now, I don't want you to buy into the ideas in this book just because of my resume. In fact, I don't think you should do that with virtually any book. I want these ideas to stand on their own merits, even if they came from a five-year-old.

This journey isn't about blindly following my words or anyone else's, regardless of their credentials. It's about sparking your curiosity, challenging your assumptions, and empowering you to make informed decisions. It's about learning to trust that nagging feeling when numbers don't make sense or advice seems too good to be true, even when it comes from so-called "experts."

How often have you been presented with financial ideas that just don't pass the eye or sniff test? You know that feeling in your gut when something doesn't quite add up, but you ignore it because, well, that's what we've been conditioned to do. We've been taught to trust the "experts" even when our instincts are screaming otherwise.

It's time to break that cycle. Whether you end up agreeing with everything in this book or not doesn't matter. What matters is that you're engaging critically with these ideas, questioning them when they don't sit right, and forging your own financial philosophy.

Remember, personal finance is just that - personal. What works for me or your neighbor might not work for you. And that's okay. The real victory is in developing the confidence to chart your own course, even if it goes against the grain of conventional wisdom.

So, as we dive into the chapters ahead, keep an open mind, but also keep your critical thinking cap firmly in place. Question everything - including what I'm telling you. Don't ignore those moments when something feels off or doesn't add up. Explore those doubts.

I don't expect you to stand on your desk exclaiming, "O Captain! My Captain!" by the end of this book. That's not the goal here. What I do hope is that these pages get you thinking for yourself. I want you to start questioning the financial advice you've been fed and find a path that works for you, regardless of what everyone else says - including me.

Let's get started, shall we? It's time to shake things up in the world of personal finance and start paying attention to those gut feelings we've been trained to ignore. Because at the end of the day, the most valuable financial tool you have isn't a fancy investment strategy, a high-yield savings account, or even a finance guru's stamp of approval. It's your ability to think independently, trust your instincts, and make choices that align with your unique goals and values.

I

The Awakening

Get ready to challenge everything you thought you knew about personal finance. Let's shake up conventional wisdom and set the stage for a radical rethinking of your relationship with money.

1

It's Not My Fault

Why This Book Isn't Your Typical Money Manual

Welcome to a book that's about to turn your financial world upside down – or at least give it a good shake. If you're looking for the same old recycled money advice that's been circulating since your grandparents' day, I'm afraid you've picked up the wrong book. But if you're ready to challenge the status quo and think critically about your finances, you're in for a treat.

What You're Getting Into

This book is the financial equivalent of coloring outside the lines. We're going to question those tried-and-true money maxims that everyone seems to parrot without a second thought. You know the "rules" that have been repeated so often they've become gospel, even though their origins are sketchy at best.

As a former financial advisor and current financial coach, I've seen firsthand how these one-size-fits-all rules can be more like one-size-fits-some. I've worked with people who've achieved remarkable success by throwing the rulebook out the window. Their stories, along with a healthy dose of skepticism and some unconventional wisdom, form the backbone of this book.

Important Disclaimers and Legal Stuff

Now, before we dive in, let's get a few things straight:

1. This book is meant to get you thinking, looking at, and considering alternatives. It's not a substitute for professional advice.
2. Before you make ANY decisions based on the ideas in this book, consult with a professional in the respective field. This includes, but is not limited to, attorneys, investment advisors, financial planners, accountants, and doctors.
3. The information provided in this book is for general informational and educational purposes only. It is not intended to be a substitute for professional advice. The author and publisher do not render legal, accounting, financial, or other professional services through this book.
4. The ideas and strategies contained in this book may not be suitable for your situation. You should always consult with a professional where appropriate.
5. While I (the author) have made every effort to provide accurate information at the time of publication, neither I nor the publisher assumes any responsibility for errors, inaccuracies, or omissions.
6. This book contains my own opinions and ideas. It is sold with the understanding that neither I nor the publisher is engaged in rendering financial, legal, or other professional services by publishing this book. The reader should consult his or her own professional advisors before adopting any version of any suggestions in this book or drawing inferences from it.
7. The use of this book implies your acceptance of this disclaimer.

The Real Goal Here

My aim isn't to replace one set of rigid rules with another. Instead, I want to spark your critical thinking. I want you to question why certain financial advice is given and whether it truly applies to your unique situation.

Remember, most big-name financial gurus got rich by selling advice to the masses, not by following their own guidance to the letter. They run businesses, leverage credit, and invest in ways that often don't align with the simple "budget, save, retire" mantra they preach.

Who This Book Is For

This book is for the rebels, the zig-zag thinkers, the innovators. It's for those who've tried conventional financial advice and found it wanting. It's for critical thinkers who aren't satisfied with "because I said so" as a reason for financial decisions.

If you're looking for unique approaches to financial freedom, if you've struggled with traditional guidance, or if you simply enjoy questioning the status quo, you're in the right place.

The Ultimate Irony

Here's the kicker: if I do my job right, you'll finish this book questioning everything in it. And I'm perfectly fine with that! The goal isn't to create a new set of unquestionable financial commandments. It's to help you develop the habit of asking "why?" when it comes to your money.

A Final Note

As you read, remember that personal finance is just that – personal. What works for one person might be a trainwreck for another. Use this book as a starting point for your own financial exploration, not as an infallible roadmap.

So, are you ready to challenge some financial orthodoxy? Great! Let's embark on this journey of financial heresy together.

2

The Rules We Never Question

The Financial Echo Chamber

Welcome to the world of personal finance, where experts routinely spout financial rules. "Save 10% of your income." "Only buy a car with cash." "Never get an adjustable-rate mortgage." Sound familiar? These financial commandments have been repeated so often they've become a sort of money mantra, echoing through the halls of banks, financial advisors' offices, and countless dinner table conversations.

But here's the kicker: How many of us have actually stopped to question these rules? To dig into their origins, examine their relevance, or consider their applicability to our unique situations? If you're like most people, the answer is probably "not often enough."

The Courage to Question

It takes a certain kind of courage to question the status quo, especially when it comes to something as important (and often intimidating) as personal finance. After all, we're all just financial simpletons. Who are we to question the wisdom of the financial sages?

Well, I'm here to tell you that not only can you question these rules, but you absolutely should. Why? Two main reasons:

1. **Time waits for no rule**. What was sound financial advice in 1980 might be as outdated as a floppy disk in today's economic landscape.
2. **One size rarely fits all**. While a rule might work great for the average Joe, you're not the average Joe. You're you, with your unique circumstances, goals, and opportunities.

The Opportunity Cost of Blind Obedience

Here's a sobering thought: You might be missing out on wealth-building opportunities simply because you're too busy following rules that don't apply to you. It's like trying to win a race while wearing someone else's shoes – they might be great shoes, but if they don't fit you, you're not going to win any medals.

I've seen it happen. Intelligent, capable people who can't seem to comprehend alternatives, let alone evaluate and perform a rough risk analysis. They can play the game of personal finance, but they're not winning. They're making moves, but they're not strategizing.

The Chess Game of Finance

Think of personal finance as a chess game. Many people learn the basic rules – how each piece moves and the objective of the game. They can play, moving pieces around the board. But that doesn't mean they see the bigger picture. They're not anticipating their opponent's moves or setting up complex strategies five turns in advance.

In finance, as in chess, the true masters are those who can think several moves ahead and who can see patterns and opportunities, whereas others see only rules and limitations.

A Lesson in Thinking Differently

Let me take you back to World War II for a moment. There was a fascinating counter-intelligence operation called Operation Mincemeat. The British planted false invasion plans on a corpse dressed as a Royal Marines officer, then allowed the body to wash up on a Spanish beach, knowing the information would make its way to German intelligence.

Now, here's the interesting part. For this operation to succeed, they needed the person who discovered this information to be not too clever. A "zig-zag thinker" might have suspected the information was false and reacted accordingly, potentially causing the worst possible outcome for the British.

But then again, a real zig-zag thinker might have realized that other zig-zag thinkers would think it was false and conclude it must be true... and on and on in an endless loop of possibilities.

The Curse and Blessing of Zig-Zag Thinking

This is both the curse and the blessing of being a zig-zag thinker. We can go down endless rabbit holes, questioning and re-questioning, analyzing from every angle. It can be exhausting. But sometimes, digging that hole ends up at the truth – or even better, a revelation.

That's exactly why I wrote this book. This is not to say that all financial rules or guidelines are bad, but to encourage you to stop taking them at face value. It's time to peel back the layers to figure out if there's anything to them or if they're just pure marketing fluff.

Is there a kernel of brilliance in these rules that can be nurtured and exploited? Or is there something contradictory about them that's holding you back? For me, there have been plenty of common financial rules that have cost me time, money, and progress.

Sacred Cows, Meet Barbecue

So, we're about to slaughter some sacred cows of personal finance. Don't worry – I don't need or even want you to agree with everything. My goal is much simpler: I want you to start understanding the questions you need to ask to figure out if a financial rule is right for you.

If this book helps you break free from artificial confines and achieve your true potential, it's done more than I dared hope for.

The Road Ahead

In the chapters that follow, we're going to dive deep into some of the most common financial rules and guidelines. We'll examine their origins, question their relevance, and consider alternatives. We'll look at real-life examples of people who've achieved success by coloring outside the lines of conventional financial wisdom.

Remember, the goal isn't to create a new set of unbreakable rules. It's to develop your critical thinking skills when it comes to your money. To help you see the chessboard of your finances more clearly, anticipate moves, and craft strategies that work for you – not for some hypothetical average person.

So, are you ready to start questioning the status quo? To think in zig-zags and see where it leads you? If you are, then let's begin.

3

Money Can Buy Happiness

Debunking the Happiness Ceiling

You've probably heard it a thousand times: "Money can't buy happiness." It's usually followed by some heartwarming story about a millionaire who's miserable or a monk who's found bliss in a cave. But let's be real for a moment. While it's true that you can't simply swipe your credit card at the Happiness Store, the idea that money and joy are unrelated is about as honest as horse feathers.

Let's talk about the famous "$75,000 happiness threshold." Studies have suggested that happiness levels off after you hit this magical income number. But here's the kicker – that doesn't mean money stops mattering after $75K. It just means you're not going to turn into a constantly giggling human emoji, bouncing off the walls with joy every time your income ticks up.

The goal isn't to be in a constant state of ecstasy. It's about eliminating stress, gaining confidence in your future, and having the freedom to add things you want to your life. And guess what? A lot of that takes money.

How Cash Crushes Your Worries

Think about the last time you were really stressed. Chances are, money (or the lack thereof) played a role. Maybe it was an unexpected car repair, a medical bill, or just the gnawing anxiety of living paycheck to paycheck.

Now, imagine a life where those financial stressors simply... disappear. That's what money can do. It's not about being able to buy a solid gold toilet (but you do you). It's about the peace of mind that comes from knowing you can handle whatever life throws at you.

Money is the ultimate stress eliminator. It's the difference between lying awake at night wondering how you'll pay the bills and sleeping soundly, knowing you're covered.

Opening Doors to Joy

Here's a radical idea: Money doesn't just eliminate bad stuff but actively enables the good stuff. Want to take that dream vacation? Money makes it happen. Passionate about a cause? Money lets you contribute meaningfully. Want to spend more time with family? Money can buy you that time.

It's not about buying happiness directly. It's about removing the barriers that stand between you and the things that bring you joy. Money is the key that unlocks the door to experiences, opportunities, and choices that contribute to a fulfilling life.

When Happiness Has a Price Tag

Here's a little experiment I like to do: Ask people what would make them truly happy. The answers might surprise you – or maybe they won't. Here's what I often hear:

- "Not struggling to pay bills every month."
- "Being able to help my parents retire comfortably."
- "Paying off my house."

- "Taking a year off work to travel or pursue a passion."
- "Sending my kids to college without drowning in debt."

Notice a pattern? The vast majority of these happiness-inducing scenarios have one thing in common: they require money—cold, hard cash.

It's a stark reminder that when we strip away the platitudes and get down to brass tacks, many of the things that would genuinely improve people's happiness are directly tied to financial resources. We're not talking about frivolous luxuries here – we're talking about fundamental aspects of a secure, fulfilling life.

This reality check puts the "money can't buy happiness" mantra in a whole new light. Sure, you can't purchase joy in a bottle (although a good bottle of wine comes pretty close), but you can certainly buy your way out of many of life's most pressing stressors and into many of its most rewarding experiences.

How Wealth Transforms Neighborhoods

Let's zoom out for a moment and look at the bigger picture. Communities with money are fundamentally different from those without. It's not just about individual happiness – it's about collective well-being.

In communities with resources, you see hope, cooperation, and progress. People have the luxury of thinking beyond mere survival. They can invest in education, start businesses, and work together to improve their shared spaces.

On the flip side, communities lacking resources often struggle with crime, desperation, and a pervasive sense of hopelessness. It's hard to focus on personal growth or community building when you're worried about putting food on the table.

Money, at a community level, creates the conditions for happiness to flourish. It's the fertile soil in which the seeds of joy can take root and grow.

Stacking the Odds in Your Favor

Here's the thing about money — it doesn't guarantee success, but it sure does improve your odds. Think of it like this: You can climb Mount Everest with basic gear and no guide, but your chances of reaching the summit (and surviving) are a lot better if you've got top-notch equipment and an experienced team.

One of my favorite movie lines is from *Ford v Ferrari* when Carroll Shelby tells Lee Iacocca, "You can't buy a win, Lee. But maybe you could buy the guy who gets you a shot." Money works the same way. It can't guarantee you'll achieve your goals, but it can give you better tools, more opportunities, and a stronger support system. It's about stacking the deck in your favor.

A Dangerous Myth

The phrase "money can't buy happiness" is well-intentioned. It's meant to remind us that there's more to life than material possessions. But taken too literally, it can be downright harmful.

When people hear "money can't buy happiness," they might conclude that they don't need money to be happy. This can lead to poor financial decisions and a lack of preparation for the future.

Think of the person who commits to being happy regardless of money and then doesn't save or invest. He ends up in retirement, realizing that he needs some money but is now unable to work. Allowing or encouraging this to happen is downright criminal.

Investing in Your Happiness

So, where does this leave us? Should we all become Gordon Gekko, proclaiming that greed is good? Not quite. But we should recognize that money is a crucial ingredient in the recipe for a happy life.

Here's your action plan:

1. Acknowledge that money matters. Don't feel guilty about wanting financial security and abundance.
2. Create a financial checklist that aligns with your vision of a happy life. What experiences or freedoms would money unlock for you?
3. Invest in your earning potential. Whether it's education, skills, or networking, increasing your income is a valid path to increasing your happiness.
4. Use money as a tool for stress reduction. Build an emergency fund, pay off debt, and create a financial cushion.
5. Think beyond yourself. Consider how your financial success could positively impact your community.

Remember, saying "money can buy happiness" doesn't mean that cash is the only ingredient. But it is a crucial one. It's the foundation upon which you can build a life filled with choice, security, and opportunity.

So the next time someone tells you money can't buy happiness, feel free to agree – then add, "But it sure can help you find it."

II

Education

Is that expensive degree really worth it? Let's explore unconventional approaches to education and career preparation that could save you a fortune. Prepare to question the ROI of traditional higher education.

4

Don't Go To College

Debunking the College Premium

Let's start with a statement that will make your high school guidance counselor fume: going to college might be the worst financial decision you ever make. Yep, I said it. I, a product of the college educational system, suggest that those hallowed halls of higher learning might not be the ticket to financial success we've all been led to believe.

Now, before you accuse me of being anti-education, hear me out. The problem isn't education itself. It's the assumption that a college degree is a guaranteed ticket to a six-figure salary and lifelong financial security. Spoiler alert: it's not.

Degrees vs. Trades

Here's a reality check: many jobs that don't require a college education can pay $100,000 a year or more. While your college-educated friends are drowning in student loan debt and fighting for entry-level positions, skilled tradespeople are out there earning six figures from day one.

Don't believe me? Just ask Mike Rowe, the champion of dirty jobs. He'll tell you about plumbers, electricians, and welders who are laughing all the way to the bank while their college-educated counterparts are still trying to figure out how to pay off their student loans.

When Education Becomes a Prison

Speaking of student loans, let's talk about the student debt crisis. We're seeing a generation of graduates who can't even afford to pay the interest on their loans, let alone the principal. They're stuck in a financial quicksand, sinking deeper with every passing year.

Compare that to someone who enters the workforce straight out of high school or after a short stint in trade school. They're debt-free, earning a solid income, and have a four-year head start on building wealth. By the time their college-educated peers are finally breaking even, they could be well on their way to financial independence.

When Brand Names Break the Bank

Now, I know what some of you are thinking. "But what about the prestige of a top-tier university?" Well, let me let you in on a little secret. That prestige comes with a hefty price tag, and the return on investment often doesn't match the cost.

The idea that attending a college that's 50 times more expensive will lead to a salary 50 times higher is a complete fantasy. In reality, many companies have standardized salary bands. Whether you went to State U or the Ivy League, you might end up making the same salary. The only difference? The size of your student loan payments.

Learning Without Lectures

Remember that line from *Good Will Hunting* about getting an education for $1.50 in late charges at the public library? In today's digital age, it's more true than ever. The internet has democratized information to an unprecedented degree.

Want to learn coding? There are free online courses. Interested in business? You can access lectures from top business schools online, often for free. The skills and knowledge that were once locked behind ivy-covered walls are now available to anyone with an internet connection and the motivation to learn.

Connections Beyond Campus

One of the biggest selling points for college is the network you'll build. But let's be real: in the age of LinkedIn and industry meetups, you don't need to spend four years and six figures to build a professional network.

I attended Northwestern University, a prestigious school with a reasonable alumni network. Want to know how many times that network has directly benefited my career or business? Zero. Real-world connections and skills have proven far more valuable than any alumni directory.

Lessons Outside the Classroom

Now, I'm not saying college doesn't provide valuable experiences. It can be a time of personal growth, self-discovery, and some epic parties (often inversely related to the cost of the school). But are those experiences worth potentially crippling debt and years of lost earnings?

Consider the experiences you could have with four years of freedom and a steady income. Travel the world. Start a business. Volunteer for causes you care about. These real-world experiences can be just as transformative as any college course and come without the burden of student loans.

Redefining Success

So, what's the alternative? It depends on your goals. If you're passionate about a field that genuinely requires a degree, by all means, pursue it. But be smart about it. Consider alternative schools. Explore online degree options.

For many, the best path might be vocational training, apprenticeships, or simply jumping into the workforce and learning on the job. The key is to approach your education and career with intention, rather than blindly following the college conveyor belt.

A Father's Change of Heart

As a parent, I've had to confront my own biases about college. A decade ago, I was dead set on my son attending university. Now? I'm increasingly open to the idea that he might be better off skipping it entirely.

If the goal is a life worth living, a fulfilling career, and financial stability, I'm no longer convinced that college is the best or only path. In fact, I'm starting to think that getting a head start on life might be the smartest move he could make.

Charting Your Own Course

Look, I'm not saying college is evil or that no one should go. What I am saying is that it's time to question the automatic assumption that college is necessary for success. It's time to consider all the options and choose the path that makes the most sense for you - financially, personally, and professionally.

Maybe that's a four-year degree. Maybe it's trade school. Maybe it's starting a business or joining the workforce right away. The point is there's no one-size-fits-all solution.

So before you sign on that dotted line for student loans, take a step back. Consider your goals, your passions, and the financial implications. Because at the end of the day, the smartest investment isn't necessarily in a degree - it's in yourself and your future.

Remember, some of the most successful people in the world - from tech titans to entertainment moguls - never finished college. They didn't let the lack of a degree hold them back, and neither should you.

Your future is too important to be left to conventional wisdom. It's time to write your own rulebook. And who knows? Skipping college might be the first chapter in your success story.

III

Career

Your approach to work might be holding you back financially. Let's examine counterintuitive career strategies that could dramatically boost your earning potential and job satisfaction. It's time to play the career game with a new set of rules.

5

Get A Job With A Pension

When the New Thing Isn't Delivering

Let's kick things off with a statement that might make you scratch your head: the good old-fashioned pension plan isn't dead. In fact, it might just be your ticket to a worry-free retirement.

Now, I know what you're thinking. "Pensions? Aren't those relics from the era of rotary phones and cassette tapes?" Well, almost, but not quite. While it's true that most companies have swapped pensions for 401(k)s, there are still jobs out there that offer this golden ticket to retirement bliss.

Pensions Still Reign Supreme

Before you dismiss the idea of finding a job with a pension as a wild goose chase, let's talk about where these gems are hiding. Firefighters, police officers, teachers - these professions often come with pension plans that would make your 401(k) jealous.

But it's not just public sector jobs. Some private companies, rare as they may be, still offer pensions. It's like finding oil in your backyard, but trust me, they exist.

When 4% Turns Into 120%

Let me throw some numbers at you that might just make you reconsider your career path. In my area, there's a network of Christian schools that offers a pension plan that'll make your jaw drop. For every year you work, you get 4% of your salary as a pension. Work for 30 years, and you're looking at 120% of your final salary in retirement.

Now, I'm no math whiz (although I did take several calculus classes), but even I can see that's a pretty sweet deal. And the best part? The school funds it entirely. That's right, not a penny comes out of your paycheck.

Retiring at 48

Do you think retiring at 48 is just a pipe dream? Think again. I've got a buddy who's a firefighter. He started right out of high school and hung up his helmet at 48 with his maximum pension (75% of his salary). While the rest of his friends are still grinding away, hoping to retire after 20 more years, he's living his best life fishing up in northern Michigan.

Now, I'm not saying you should rush out and become a firefighter (unless, of course, you want to). But it's worth considering how a pension could dramatically change your retirement timeline.

Uncle Sam is Changing His Tune

Now, here's where things get interesting. Even the military, long known for its stellar pension plan, is shifting gears. New recruits are now offered a 401(k)-style plan instead of the traditional pension.

But here's the kicker: this change only highlights how valuable those remaining pension plans are. If you can snag a job that still offers one, you're getting something that's increasingly rare and precious.

A Lower Salary Might Actually Be More

Here's where it gets really juicy. When you're job hunting, don't just look at the salary. A lower-paying job with a pension might actually leave you better off in the long run than a higher-paying job without one.

It's not just about your lifestyle now. It's about your lifestyle when you're old and gray. A defined benefit pension gives you something most of us can only dream of — predictable, guaranteed income in retirement.

Turning One Pension into Two

Now, let me tell you a little secret. Many pension holders have figured out a way to game the system (legally, of course). They work long enough to vest in one pension, then move to another state and start all over again.

Imagine retiring with not just one but two or even three pensions. It's like hitting the retirement jackpot multiple times. And while it might not be easy, it's certainly not impossible.

When "Hoping" Turns into "Knowing"

Here's the real kicker: peace of mind. While the rest of us are crossing our fingers and hoping our 401(k)s will be enough and praying that the stock market soars, pension-holders know exactly what they're getting in retirement.

It's the difference between hoping you can afford to retire and knowing you can. And let me tell you, that peace of mind is priceless.

Don't Dismiss the Pension

Look, I get it. In today's job market, finding a position with a pension might seem as likely as finding a Blockbuster. But they're out there, and they're worth looking for.

So the next time you're job hunting, don't just look at the salary and the

401(k) match. Ask about pensions. You might be surprised at what you find. And if you do stumble upon a job with a solid pension plan? Grab it with both hands, and don't let go.

Because in the world of retirement planning, a good pension isn't just a nice-to-have. It might just be your secret weapon for a worry-free retirement.

Remember, your grandpa might have been onto something with his pension plan. Sometimes, the old ways are the best ways. And when it comes to securing your financial future, a pension might just be the blast from the past you need.

6

Switch Jobs Frequently

Debunking the Stay-Put Mentality

When it comes to career advice, I usually recommend focusing on doing your job well and playing a bit of office politics. However, it's important to recognize that this approach, while professionally admirable, may not always lead to the promotions and raises you deserve. This is where switching companies is a crucial strategy in your career playbook.

By excelling in your current role, you're building a solid reputation and skill set. But even with handsome raises, there may be a time when your company fails to recognize your true value. That's when it's time to take that value to the open market. Job-hopping isn't about being disloyal; it's about being smart with your career and financial future.

Remember when staying with one company for 40 years was the gold standard of career success? Well, it's time to wake up and smell the 21st-century coffee. That ship hasn't just sailed; it's sunk to the bottom of the corporate ocean.

Your grandparents might have clocked in at the same place from their first day until retirement, but let's face it, loyalty is often preached instead of practiced. Times have changed, and so should your career strategy.

A One-Way Street to Nowhere

Have you ever heard a company say it treats its employees like family? Let me translate that for you: "We expect loyalty but don't expect it in return."

Here's a hard truth: no company is splitting profits equally, no matter how much they preach about employee value. You're not a cherished family member. You're a name on a roster. And in big corporations? You're not even a name - you're an employee number with a price tag.

Why Staying Put Keeps You Poor

Let's talk about raises. You just got a 10% bump, and you're feeling pretty good. Well, I'm about to rain on your parade. If the market rate for your position is 20% higher than what you're making, that 10% raise is just a consolation prize.

Companies have a dirty little secret: they'd rather you leave and hire someone new at market rate than give you the raise you deserve. It doesn't make any financial sense, but that's your corporate logic.

Numbers Don't Lie

Still not convinced? Let's dive into some stats that'll make your head spin:

1. **Wage Warriors**: Job switchers see wage increases of 5.8% to 6.4% on average, while loyal employees get a measly 3%. That's like choosing between a steak dinner and a value menu burger.
2. **Promotion Express**: Employees who switch jobs are 67% more likely to move up the ladder. Staying put? You might as well be on a corporate treadmill.
3. **Skill Sellers' Market**: In hot fields like tech and healthcare, switching jobs can net you a 10-20% salary boost. You might even snag a nice signing bonus. That's not pocket change; that's vacation-in-the-Bahamas money.

4. **Lifetime Earnings Bonanza**: Strategic job hoppers could see a 15-30% increase in lifetime earnings. We're talking hundreds of thousands, maybe even millions more, over your career. That's the difference between retiring on a beach and retiring on your couch.
5. **The Compound Effect**: Each job switch with a 10-20% raise isn't just a one-time win; it's the gift that keeps on giving. Future raises will be based on that higher salary, creating a snowball effect that could boost your lifetime income by 30-50%.

Job-Hopping Success

Let me tell you about my friend Ronald. He's no Steve Jobs or Elon Musk - just an average Joe with an extraordinary strategy. Every 3-5 years, like clockwork, Ronald packs up his desk and moves to a new company. Each move comes with a better title, a fatter paycheck, and a signing bonus that would make your eyes water.

The result? Ronald's resume reads like a Who's Who of top companies. He's been featured in magazines, rose to executive positions, and lives a lifestyle that would make a rockstar jealous. And remember, this is a guy with no special skills, no unique degree, just a relentless commitment to upgrading his position.

When potential employers see Ronald's history of prestigious companies and ever-increasing titles, they assume he must be the cream of the crop. And you know what? In a way, he is - because he's absolutely mastered the art of the job hop.

Why You're Stuck in a Rut

Meanwhile, you're sitting in your cubicle, working overtime, being told there's not enough in the budget for raises this year. Maybe they throw you a bone, saying you got a little more than your colleagues. Congratulations, you've just won the "Corporate Sucker of the Year" award. You figure that, eventually, they'll reward you properly.

Your sense of loyalty is a one-way ticket to financial mediocrity. Every day you stay put is a day you're leaving money on the table. That warm, fuzzy feeling of company loyalty? It's not paying your bills or funding your retirement.

Hop Your Way to the Top

Look, I'm not saying you should switch jobs every six months. But if you're not reassessing your position in the job market every couple of years, you're doing yourself a massive disservice.

Here's your new career mantra: Assess, Excel, and Exit.

1. **Assess**: Know your market value. Websites like Glassdoor and salary.com will give the real scoop that your company won't.
2. **Excel**: Give your current job your all. Build skills, make connections, and leave a stellar impression.
3. **Exit**: When you've maxed out your growth and compensation potential, it's time to move on.

Remember, in today's job market, stability doesn't come from a single long-term employer. It comes from being adaptable, continually upgrading your skills, and being willing to make a move when the right opportunity comes along.

So, the next time you're tempted to settle in for the long haul at your current job, ask yourself: Am I really moving forward, or am I just standing still while the world passes me by?

Your career is a journey, not a destination. Keep moving, keep growing, and watch your bank account grow along with you. After all, in the game of career chess, the most valuable piece is the one that can move the most.

7

Only Rent An Apartment

The Homeownership Myth

Rent an apartment? You might say, "But Pete, I want to build equity. I want to secure my financial future by owning an asset. Isn't that the American dream?" We could certainly debate that (and will in a later chapter), but if you're aiming to be competitive in your career, renting gives you a huge advantage.

Mobile Renters

Between the people I know who have bought homes and those who have rented and remained flexible for career opportunities, there's no question: the renters who stayed mobile and seized opportunities have not only done better financially but have often secured their financial independence midway through their careers. In contrast, those who bought a home, settled into a job at a company, and limited themselves to local job markets often find themselves constrained by geography. They can only work within a smaller pool of businesses and industries that happen to be nearby.

The Power of Mobility

From Entry-Level to Seven Figures

Let me tell you about my friend who moved from Chicago to Seattle to California, receiving better job opportunities with each move. In his first twenty years, he went from an entry-level position to a seven-figure annual salary with stock options, exposure, and influence that put him in the company of celebrities and industry leaders.

Million-Dollar Net Worth in Five Years

Another friend moved from Detroit to a small tech company out West, bouncing between four different companies in five years, accumulating stock options along the way, and achieving a multimillion-dollar net worth, ensuring that neither he nor his children would ever need to work again.

The Downside of Homeownership

On the flip side, I've seen people plant their roots early because of family commitments, a first job offer, or a loyalty to a specific industry. They buy a house and settle in, and decades later, they're still working to pay off their mortgage, scraping by, and hoping to secure a middle-management position.

Benefits of Renting for Career Advancement

1. Flexibility to exploit career opportunities
2. Reduced competition pool
3. Ability to move with market trends
4. Potential for significant salary and compensation increases
5. Access to ownership stakes and stock options
6. Increased visibility with corporate leadership

Big Opportunities for Renters

Renting doesn't guarantee these outcomes, but it provides flexibility to move wherever the opportunities are. Even seemingly small sacrifices, like delaying homeownership, can be disproportionately rewarded in the long run. Those sacrifices may allow you to eventually own the home of your dreams, completely paid off, in much less time than you would have imagined.

Short-Term Sacrifice for Long-Term Gain

Renting, rather than buying, can free you from making decisions based on attachment to property. It opens you up to extreme dislocations in the job market, where companies are willing to overpay for scarce talent. The flexibility of renting can lead to accelerated career growth and financial success, potentially allowing you to achieve your homeownership goals faster than the traditional methods.

8

Never Work Just One Job

A Cautionary Tale

Remember Enron? No, I'm not about to launch into a boring corporate ethics lecture. I want you to think about the Enron employees for a moment. These folks had it all. They collected steady paychecks, 401(k)s loaded with company stock, bonuses, stock options, and neighborhoods full of colleagues. The idyllic suburban life.

Until it wasn't.

When Enron collapsed, these employees lost everything - their income, retirement savings, bonuses, and even their home values. It was a brutal lesson in the dangers of putting all your eggs in one basket.

Now, you might be thinking, "But I don't work for a shady energy company!" Fair enough. But let me ask you this: How different is your situation, really?

The System is Rigged

Here's a hard truth. The system is broken. These days, you need a six-figure salary just to be considered middle-class. Home prices are through the roof, education costs are skyrocketing, and don't even get me started on healthcare. You're not just paying for food, shelter, and clothing anymore - you're financing a whole lifestyle that previous generations couldn't even imagine.

And here's the kicker: Your income isn't magically going to keep up. If you're waiting for that big promotion to fix everything, your employer owns you. While you're putting in "just a few more years," inflation is eating away at your purchasing power.

You need a fix, and you need it today. That's where the side hustle comes in.

Finding Your 5-Hour Solution

We've all bought into this idea that a 40-hour workweek is the norm. But who says you can't use those other hours to get ahead? I'm not talking about burning yourself out with 80-hour weeks. I'm talking about finding just five extra hours each week to transform your financial future.

Five hours is just one hour a day, Monday to Friday. Or you can knock out a couple of hours on the weekend. It's the difference between getting by and getting ahead.

7 Reasons to Start Today

1. **Cash, Cash, Cash**: Extra income means extra opportunities. Pay off debt, boost your savings, or finally take that vacation without guilt.
2. **Level Up Your Career**: Your side hustle can be a laboratory for new skills. Learn social media marketing by promoting your Etsy shop, or hone your leadership skills by organizing local events.
3. **Flexibility is Freedom**: Unlike your 9-to-5, your side hustle bends to your schedule. Work when you want, where you want.
4. **Find Your Purpose**: Sometimes, your day job is just that - a job. Your side hustle can be your passion project, giving you that sense of fulfillment you crave.
5. **Network Like a Boss**: Every client, every customer, and every collabo-

ration is a new connection. You're not just making money but building a web of opportunities.
6. **Entrepreneur in Training**: Today's side hustle could be tomorrow's empire. It's your low-risk launch pad into the world of entrepreneurship that could be the next Apple or Under Armour (both started as side hustles).
7. **Diversify Your Life**: Like your investment portfolio, your income streams should be diversified. When one stream dries up, the others keep you afloat.

Trial and Error in Action

Now, let me get personal for a moment. I've been tinkering with side hustles since I landed my first "real" job. Some were great, others were epic losers.

I've sold hot dogs at the horse races. I've handed out water bottles at the speedway. I've mowed more lawns than I can count. I've tried my hand at freelance writing and calligraphy and even dabbled in dropshipping.

But you know what? Each of those "flameouts" taught me something. They helped me refine my skills, understand my interests, and figure out what I really wanted from a side hustle.

Today, I've found my sweet spot creating online content. It fits my skills and aligns with my interests, and I can ramp it up or dial it back depending on what's going on in my life. It's not for everyone, but it's perfect for me.

Finding Your Side Hustle Soulmate

Here's the thing: My perfect side hustle probably isn't your perfect side hustle. Maybe you're the next hot dog king of your local stadium. Maybe you've got a knack for lawn care, like my buddy Jason Crisp. His neighbors swear he installed artificial grass.

The key is to start trying. Yes, you're going to have some duds. You might waste a few weekends on projects that go nowhere. But each attempt gets you closer to finding that side hustle that clicks.

Your Financial Future is in Your (Side) Hands

Look, I get it. Starting a side hustle can seem daunting. You're already busy, already tired, already stretched thin. But here's the reality. Your financial future is in your hands. No one's going to swoop in and save the day. There's no government bailout to grant you a comfortable retirement.

Your side hustle is your financial life jacket in a sea of economic uncertainty. It's your ticket to a future where you're not just surviving but thriving.

So, what are you waiting for? Those five hours a week aren't going to fill themselves. It's time to roll up your sleeves, try out some ideas, and find your side hustle soulmate. Trust me, when it clicks, you'll wish you started earlier.

Remember, in the world of side hustles, the only real failure is never starting. So get out there and start hustling. Your financial freedom is counting on it.

IV

Spending

Penny-pinching isn't always the path to wealth. Let's explore when spending more can actually improve your financial health. Get ready to give yourself permission to indulge – strategically.

9

Buy That Gourmet Coffee

The Great Coffee Debate

You've heard it a thousand times: "Want to get rich? Stop buying fancy coffee!" It's the battle cry of wannabe financial gurus everywhere, painting your daily macchiato as the villain in your financial story. But what if I told you that your coffee habit isn't the budget-busting demon it's made out to be? Let's dive into why that premium coffee might actually be a smart part of your financial diet.

The Myth of the $300,000 Latte

First, let's address the often exaggerated math. You've probably seen those eye-popping calculations: "Skip your daily $5 latte and retire with an extra $300,000!" Sounds great, right? But here's the catch: these numbers are nonsense.

These calculations assume you're not only skipping that coffee but also investing that $5 every single day, without fail, for decades. They also conveniently ignore the fact that making coffee at home isn't free. Between beans, equipment, and your precious time, home brewing comes with its own price tag. Sure, it might be cheaper, but we're not talking about going from

$5 a day to zero.

Coffee Isn't Breaking the Bank

Let's look at some actual data. According to a July 2022 survey by Statista, 81.1% of people spend less than $40 a month at coffee shops. That's right, less than $40. More than half spend under $20. To put that in perspective, it's a drop in the bucket compared to major expenses like housing, food, or even your monthly smartphone bill.

If you're struggling financially, I can almost guarantee it's not because of your coffee habit. It's more likely due to larger issues in your budget – think housing costs, debt, or maybe that car payment that's a bit too hefty.

The Hidden Costs of Home Brewing

Now, don't get me wrong – making coffee at home can save you money. But it's not the financial panacea it's often made out to be. Those fancy home brewing setups? They're not cheap. Even if you choose a more affordable option like a Keurig or Nespresso, you're looking at about $1 per cup when you factor in the machine, pods, and maintenance.

And let's not forget the most valuable resource of all: your time. For many of us, especially those juggling kids, jobs, and a million other responsibilities, the convenience of grabbing a coffee on the go is worth every penny.

The Starbucks Stereotype

According to financial pundits, Starbucks is the poster child for unnecessary spending. But here's something interesting: Starbucks isn't actually targeting the financially irresponsible, or it would be facing a constantly diminishing customer base. Their core demographic? Affluent, high-income earners, urban dwellers, and health-conscious individuals. In other words, people who can afford that extra splash in their cup.

This isn't to say everyone buying premium coffee is wealthy, but it does challenge the notion that premium coffee drinkers are all one purchase away from financial ruin.

Coffee as an Experience

Here's something the budget-slashers often miss: coffee isn't just about the caffeine. For many, it's an experience. It's the comfort of a familiar ritual, a moment of peace in a hectic day, or a chance to connect with friends.

Think about it. Meeting a friend for coffee can be a much more budget-friendly social option than going out for meals or drinks. At $5 a cup, it's a relatively cheap ticket to a comfortable environment and good company. In that light, your mocha looks less like a luxury and more like a savvy social investment.

The Time-Money Trade-Off

In our busy lives, time is often more valuable than money. For many, the convenience of buying coffee rather than making it is a worthwhile trade-off. It's not just about the coffee; it's about buying yourself a few extra minutes in the morning or avoiding one more thing on your to-do list.

This time-money trade-off is a fundamental principle of personal finance that often gets overlooked in the rush to cut costs. Sometimes, spending a little more to save time is the smarter financial move.

Where to Really Look for Savings

If you're serious about improving your financial health, it's time to think bigger than your coffee cup. Look at the heavy hitters in your budget:

1. **Housing**: Are you overspending on rent or mortgage?
2. **Transportation**: Is your car payment eating up too much of your income?
3. **Debt**: Are high-interest credit card balances draining your wealth?

4. **Insurance**: Are you overpaying for coverage you don't need?

These are the areas where small changes can lead to big savings – much more than you'd get from switching to freeze-dried instant coffee.

Enjoy Your Java

Here's my take: if you enjoy your premium coffee and it fits within a reasonable budget, keep sipping. Life's too short for bad coffee, especially if that daily cup brings you joy and doesn't derail your larger financial goals.

That said, be smart about it. Perhaps you can find a loyalty program that rewards your regular visits. And yes, mixing in some home brewing can help balance things out.

The key is to look at your coffee spending in the context of your overall financial picture. If you're meeting your savings goals, paying down debt, and living within your means, then that latte isn't just acceptable – it might be a well-deserved treat.

Brew Your Own Financial Path

Personal finance is just that – personal. What works for one person might not work for another. The "latte factor" might be a useful wake-up call for some, but for many, it's an oversimplification of complex financial realities.

Instead of blindly following one-size-fits-all advice, take a holistic look at your finances. Make informed decisions based on your unique situation, values, and goals. And if that means enjoying a well-crafted cappuccino now and then, so be it.

Remember, the goal of good financial management isn't just to save money – it's to build a life you enjoy, both now and in the future. Sometimes, that life includes a really good cup of coffee.

10

Increase Your Spending

When Frugality Becomes Folly

Now, here's something that would make Dave Ramsey let out his trademark sigh. Sometimes, the smart financial move is to increase your spending. Yes, I am giving you permission - encouraging you actually - to spend more money.

The problem with most budgeting advice is that it treats every dollar the same. It's all about slashing expenses across the board as if your lawncare budget and your life-enriching vacation fund are somehow equivalent.

When Saving Loses Joy

Here's a scenario I've seen play out more times than I can count: My client, Katie, loves grabbing dinner with her friends every weekend. It's her stress relief, her social lifeline, her joy. But in the name of "responsible budgeting," she's considering cutting this expense by 15%.

Sound reasonable? Wrong. That 15% cut means Katie misses out on one weekend of fun per month. It's the difference between a fulfilling social life and a nagging sense of FOMO. And for what? A few dollars saved that probably won't make a dent in her long-term financial goals.

Identifying Your Joy Generators

Here's where it gets interesting: not all expenses are created equal. Some bring you immense joy and value, while others are almost necessary evils. The key is to identify your "joy generators" - those expenses that disproportionately contribute to your happiness and well-being.

For Katie, it was her weekend outings. For another client, Tom, it was travel. Tom lived for his annual big trip, exploring new cultures and creating memories that lasted a lifetime. Cutting his travel budget by even 5% would have meant sacrificing experiences he deeply valued.

Spending More to Live Better

So, what did I do with Katie and Tom? We increased their budgets for these joy-generating activities. Shocking, I know. But here's the thing: by allowing Katie an extra 20% for her social outings and Tom an additional 15% for his travel, we dramatically improved their quality of life.

Katie could now enjoy her weekends guilt-free, knowing she had the financial bandwidth to fully participate in her social life. Tom could extend his trip by a day or two or splurge on that special experience he'd otherwise skip. The result? Happier, more fulfilled clients who actually stuck to their budgets because they didn't feel deprived.

When Penny-Pinching Backfires

Here's a dirty little secret in the world of personal finance: excessive frugality can backfire. When you constantly deprive yourself in the name of saving money, you're setting yourself up for failure. It's like going on a crash diet - eventually, you're going to crack and binge.

By allowing yourself to spend more on what truly matters to you, you're creating a sustainable financial lifestyle. You're acknowledging your human needs and desires while still maintaining overall financial responsibility.

Finding Money in the Margins

Now, I'm not suggesting you inflate your entire budget. That's a one-way ticket to lifestyle creep and financial instability. The key is selective increases coupled with strategic decreases.

While we increased Katie's social budget and Tom's travel fund, we also found areas where they could cut back without feeling the pinch. Maybe it's switching to a cheaper cell phone plan, changing insurance companies, or finding a more affordable gym membership. The point is to reallocate funds from low-impact areas to high-joy activities.

When Spending More Saves You Money

Here's a counterintuitive truth: sometimes, spending more now can save you money in the long run. Take home maintenance, for example. Increasing your budget for regular upkeep and minor repairs can prevent costly major repairs down the line. Or consider those active trips that keep you in shape now and prevent health issues later, saving money over time.

The same principle applies to experiences. By fully funding that vacation or hobby, you're less likely to feel the need for costly "retail therapy" or impulse purchases to fill an emotional void.

From Budgeting to Value-Based Financial Planning

What I'm advocating for here isn't reckless spending. It's mindful allocation of resources based on what truly brings value to your life. It's about moving from a traditional budget to a value-based financial plan.

This approach requires honest self-reflection. What activities, experiences, or items genuinely enhance your life? Where do you get the most bang for your buck in terms of happiness and fulfillment? These are the areas where a budget increase might be not just acceptable but advisable.

Your Money, Your Values

Look, I'm not telling you to throw financial caution to the wind. What I am saying is this: your budget should reflect your values, not just your expenses. It should be a tool for living your best life, not just an ever-tightening financial straitjacket.

So take a hard look at your spending. Where are you shortchanging your happiness in the name of savings? Where could a modest increase in spending lead to a significant boost in life satisfaction?

Remember, the goal of good financial management isn't to die with the biggest bank account. It's to create a life of balance, joy, and financial security. Sometimes, that means giving yourself permission to spend a little more on what truly matters.

After all, life's too short to always choose the cheapest option on the menu. With thoughtful budget increases in the right areas, you can have your financial cake and eat it too.

11

Play The Lottery

Challenging the Anti-Lottery Orthodoxy

Care to know how I enrage financial experts? I let them know that I don't care if you play the lottery. In fact, buying a lottery ticket might not be the financial sin it's often made out to be.

Now, before you accuse me of going off the deep end, let's get real. I'm not saying you should mortgage your house to buy Powerball tickets. What I am saying is that in moderation, lottery play can be a form of entertainment with a potentially life-changing upside.

When Small Splurges Make Sense

Let's talk again about that daily premium coffee that financial experts are always vilifying. Some people could be spending $100 a month. Now, compare that to the average lottery spend of $50 a month. Suddenly, those lottery tickets don't seem so extravagant, do they?

Here's the kicker: in many states, you can play for a chance at a seven-figure jackpot for as little as a dollar. That's less than the cost of a gumball from those machines at the grocery store exit. And let's be honest, which one has the potential to change your life?

When Losing is Still Winning

Remember the last time the Mega Millions hit a billion dollars? I chipped in a few bucks for the office pool. Sure, we all joked about our slim chances, but for a couple of days, we got to daydream about early retirement and private islands.

That shared experience, the collective "what if," the laughter and camaraderie – that's worth something. It's entertainment, pure and simple. And at a few bucks a pop, it's cheaper than a movie ticket.

When Lightning Does Strike

Now, I know what you're thinking. "But the odds are astronomical!" And you're right. The chances of winning big are slimmer than your chances of becoming a professional athlete or dating a supermodel.

But here's the thing: people do win. I had a friend who snagged several hundred thousand dollars from a lottery ticket. No, it wasn't "never work again" money, but it was "buy a house outright" money. It was a real financial head start that most people can only dream of.

Is it likely to happen to you? No. Is it possible? Yes.

Lottery as Stress Relief

Let's talk about stress for a moment. Financial stress, in particular, can be crushing. It can keep you up at night, strain your relationships, and impact your health. Now, I'm not suggesting that playing the lottery will solve your financial problems. I can almost guarantee you that it won't. But that dollar ticket represents hope, a tiny possibility of a life-changing event.

For many people, however small, that glimmer of hope provides a mental release. It's a way to dream big without risking big. And sometimes, that's exactly what we need to keep pushing forward.

Choosing Your Financial Drips

Here's another hard truth: no matter how tight your budget, there are always small leaks. Maybe it's that impulse buy at the checkout counter or the vending machine snack at work. These mini-splurges are part of being human.

So, if you're going to have a small financial leak (and trust me, you will), why not make it one that at least has the upside potential? That ice cream cone might satisfy your sweet tooth but won't pay off your car or mortgage.

Keeping it in Perspective

Now, let's be clear: I'm not advocating for irresponsible gambling. If you're spending rent money on lottery tickets, we need to have a different conversation. The key here is moderation and perspective.

A couple of dollars a week on lottery tickets, if it fits in your budget, isn't going to derail your financial future. But it could, however unlikely, dramatically improve it. It's about balancing the unlikely potential reward against the very limited risk.

Measuring Joy Per Dollar

Think about other forms of entertainment you indulge in. A night at the movies, a fancy coffee, a magazine subscription. How much joy do you get per dollar spent?

Now, think about the lottery ticket. For a dollar, you get to spend time imagining a different life. You get to ask, "What if?" and let your mind wander to all the possibilities. In terms of minutes of entertainment per dollar spent, the lottery might just be one of the best deals around.

A Balanced Approach to Lottery Play

Look, I'm not telling you to run out and blow your paycheck on scratch-offs. Here's what I am saying. If you enjoy playing the lottery and can do so responsibly within your budget, don't let the financial purists make you feel guilty about it.

A few dollars a week on lottery tickets isn't going to make or break your financial future. But it might just make your present situation a little more enjoyable. And who knows? You might just be that one-in-a-million winner.

If the occasional lottery ticket brings you joy and hope without jeopardizing your financial stability, that's a valid choice.

So go ahead and buy that ticket if you want to. Dream big. Just do it responsibly. After all, life's too short to always play it safe. Sometimes, a dollar and a dream is a perfectly reasonable investment in your own happiness.

12

Make That Impulse Purchase

When Saving Costs You Joy

Let's start with a statement that I haven't seen anyone else make yet: impulse purchases can be good for you. Splurging could be your taste of real freedom.

Now, I am not trying to sabotage your financial future, but let's think about it. The problem with most financial advice is that it treats you like a robot programmed to save and invest with ruthless efficiency. But here's the thing: you're human. And humans have wants, needs, and impulses.

Chasing the Unlimited Checkbook Dream

We've all fantasized about being so wealthy that you can buy whatever you want, whenever you want. See a shiny new car? It's yours. Fancy beach house? Why not? Private jet? Don't mind if I do.

This feeling of unlimited financial freedom is the holy grail of wealth. But let's face it: most of us aren't going to reach Elon Musk's level of wealth anytime soon. So, how can we capture a slice of that freedom without the billions?

Enter the concept of "freedom money."

Bringing Back Childhood Financial Bliss

Remember your childhood allowance? That magical money that appeared in your hands, free from the burden of bills, mortgages, or adult responsibilities? Every cent was yours to spend as you pleased, whether on comic books, candy, or saving up for that popular toy.

That is the feeling we're aiming to recreate. We're not doing it with your entire paycheck (sorry, but adulting and bills aren't going anywhere) but with a small, deliberate portion of your income.

Carving Out Your Financial Happy Place

Here's how it works. Once you've covered your necessities and your responsible adult financial goals (yes, keep contributing to that retirement account), carve out a small portion of your remaining income. This is your freedom money.

It might be $10 a week, $100 a month, or more if you're fortunate. The amount isn't as important as the principle: this money is yours to spend, guilt-free, on whatever your heart desires.

When Small Splurges Add Up to Joy

We've already debunked the "skip the latte, become a millionaire" spiel. But let's expand on that concept. What if that latte is exactly what you need to make it through your Monday morning meeting? What if it's a spontaneous lunch outing with your coworkers? What if your child discovers their dream toy on a family outing? What if that small indulgence is the difference between feeling powerless and feeling empowered?

Your freedom money is your ticket to these small joys. It's permission to buy that meal, that gift, or even that impulse vacation without a side of guilt. By allowing yourself controlled splurges, you're creating a sustainable financial lifestyle. You're acknowledging your human needs and desires while still maintaining overall financial responsibility.

When Small Freedom Leads to Big Rewards

Here's a secret the strict budgeters won't tell you: your freedom money can actually grow into something substantial. Maybe you don't splurge every week. That unspent freedom money accumulates, allowing for bigger purchases down the line.

Suddenly, that impulse purchase isn't so impulsive. It's a planned indulgence funded by your accumulated freedom money. It's the best of both worlds: the joy of spontaneity with the security of planning.

Turning Impulse into Intention

By designating freedom money, you're not just giving yourself permission to spend. You're creating a framework for more mindful consumption. When you know you have a specific amount to splurge, you become more intentional about how you use it.

Maybe you skip the small impulse buys in favor of saving up for something bigger. Or perhaps you find more joy in frequent tiny indulgences. Either way, you're making active choices about your spending rather than mindlessly following a restrictive budget or succumbing to every fleeting desire.

Faking It Till You Make It

Here's the beautiful thing about freedom money: it gives you a taste of that coveted financial freedom, regardless of your current wealth status. No, you can't buy a yacht. Neither can I. But you can buy that book you've been eyeing without consulting your spreadsheet first.

This feeling of financial autonomy, even in small doses, can be incredibly motivating. It reminds you why you're working hard and saving in other areas of your life. It's a reward for your financial diligence and an incentive to keep making smart money moves.

Embrace the Power of Planned Impulsivity

I'm not telling you to throw your budget out the window and go on a shopping spree. What I am saying is this: building a little room for impulse and indulgence in your financial plan isn't just okay – it's smart.

Your freedom money allowance is an investment in your financial well-being and your quality of life. It's a way to enjoy the present while still planning for the future. It's a reminder that money is a tool for living, not just a number in your bank account.

So go ahead, set up that freedom fund. Give yourself permission to make the occasional impulse purchase. Enjoy that meal, buy that wine, that book, or that spontaneous weekend getaway. Your wallet can handle it – and your soul will thank you for it.

13

Don't Go Grocery Shopping

When Saving Pennies Costs You Dollars

Experts are constantly telling us to stop eating out and that no one takes advantage of the grocery stores anymore. Well, I'm here to say that maybe you shouldn't grocery shop at all.

Now, I don't want you to starve, and I certainly don't want you to go broke. However, the problem with traditional grocery shopping isn't just the money you spend – it's the time you waste. And in our modern, fast-paced world, time might just be the most valuable currency of all.

When Bargain Hunting Becomes Expensive

It's Saturday afternoon, and you finally have some time to run to the grocery store. You're armed with a meticulously crafted shopping list, a stack of coupons, and the determination to score the best deals. Fast forward three hours, and you're trudging out of the store, exhausted, with a cart full of groceries and a significantly lighter wallet.

But there's a nagging question haunting your mind. What else could you have done with those three hours? Spent quality time with your family? Worked on that side hustle? Hit the gym? When you factor in the opportunity cost of your time, suddenly, those bargains don't look so cheap after all.

Convenience Meets Cost-Effectiveness

Let's discuss the meal kit delivery service. Now, I know what you're thinking. "Aren't those just for rich people who can't boil water?" Not anymore. The meal kit industry has evolved, and there are now options to fit almost any budget.

Take EveryPlate, for example. With meals starting at an astounding $1.99 per serving, it's not just competitive with home cooking – it might actually be cheaper. Are you currently feeding your family of four with your groceries for $8 per meal? And that's before you factor in the time and stress you save.

Or consider Dinnerly, another budget-friendly option at around $5 per serving. These services prove that convenience doesn't have to come with a luxury price tag.

When Cheap Ingredients Get Expensive

Here's something the coupon clippers don't tell you: cooking from scratch isn't always cheaper. Sure, that bag of flour might cost less than a prepared meal. But what about all the other ingredients you need to buy? What about the spices you'll use once and forget about? The produce that wilts before you can use it all?

Meal kits eliminate food waste by providing exactly what you need for each recipe. No more sad, forgotten vegetables lurking in the back of your fridge.

Reclaiming Your Most Valuable Asset

Let's talk about the most precious resource you have: time. If you're a working parent, every minute counts. Between job responsibilities, childcare or school, and trying to maintain some semblance of a social life, who has time to plan meals, shop for groceries, and cook from scratch every night?

Meal kits give you back those hours—no more meal planning. No more grocery store runs. No more staring blankly into the fridge, wondering what to cook. That time savings? It's priceless.

Becoming a Kitchen Whiz Without Culinary School

Here's a secret. Meal kits can make you a better cook. Services like Blue Apron don't just send you ingredients; they teach you cooking techniques, introduce you to new flavors, and expand your culinary horizons.

Think of it as a cooking school delivered to your door. And unlike that dusty cookbook on your shelf, you're actually putting these skills into practice.

When Convenience Food Isn't Junk Food

Let's address the elephant in the room: health. Isn't home cooking supposed to be healthier than prepared meals? Not necessarily. Many meal kit services prioritize nutrition, offering balanced meals with plenty of fruits and vegetables.

Plus, with preportioned ingredients, you're less likely to overeat. No more "cleaning your plate" of giant restaurant-sized portions.

Dinner Without the Drama

Here's something they don't teach you in financial certification classes: the value of a stress-free dinner time. End the arguments about what to cook. No more last-minute grocery store runs. Just relax with a delicious, home-cooked meal without the hassle.

This can be a game-changer for couples and families. Imagine actually enjoying the process of making and eating dinner together rather than viewing it as yet another chore.

Meal Kits on Your Terms

Now, I'm not saying you need to use meal kits for every single meal. The beauty of these services is their flexibility. Use them when you're busy, supplement with your own cooking when you have time, and order out when you feel like it.

It's about having options and making choices that work for your lifestyle and budget. With options as low as $1.99 per serving, you can even use meal kits for your everyday dining.

Rethinking the Cost of Convenience

Look, I get it. The idea of outsourcing your grocery shopping and meal planning might feel like a luxury. But when you crunch the numbers – factoring in the cost of your time, the waste from unused groceries, and the mental energy spent on meal planning – meal kits start to look less like an indulgence and more like a smart financial decision.

So here's my challenge to you: try a meal kit service for a month. Start with a budget-friendly option like EveryPlate or Dinnerly. Keep track of what you spend, but also note how much time you save and how your stress levels change. You might just find that those delivered boxes of ingredients are delivering something even more valuable: a better quality of life.

Remember, good financial planning isn't just about pinching pennies. It's about allocating your resources – both money and time – in a way that maximizes your well-being and happiness. And if that means trading your shopping cart for a meal kit subscription, well, that might just be the smartest swap you ever make.

14

Never Buy A $3,000 Car

The Siren Song of the Bargain Beater

We've all been there. You're scrolling through used car listings, and suddenly, there it is: a car for just $3,000. Your heart races, your palms get sweaty, and you start imagining all the money you'll save. But hold your horses, bargain hunter. That $3,000 car might end up costing you more than you ever imagined.

Let's dive into why that cheap car might not be the deal of the century and why it could drive your finances into a ditch.

When Cheap Gets Expensive

Here's a little economics lesson for you. Imagine a graph where one line represents the price of a car over time (trending downward), and another represents the cost of repairs (trending upward). Eventually, these lines cross. What you're left with is a car at the bottom of the price line but way up on the cost line.

In high school, we called this a "shitbox." It was fine when your feet could touch the road through the rusted floorboards, and Mom could drive you to school when the engine inevitably exploded. But when you're the mom (or dad), and this is your only ride, you're in trouble.

The Money Pit on Wheels

That $3,000 car isn't just a vehicle; it's a ticking time bomb for your wallet. Every squeak, rattle, and mysterious odor is potentially hundreds of dollars in repairs. Before you know it, you're on a first-name basis with your mechanic, and your car has its own line item in your monthly budget.

It's like adopting a high-maintenance pet. Sure, the initial cost was low, but now you're paying for premium food, vet bills, and replacing all the furniture it destroyed. Except pets are for fun, not for getting to work on time.

The Reliability Roulette

Speaking of getting to work, how much do you value actually arriving at your destination? With a $3,000 car, your daily commute becomes an adventure - and not the fun kind. Will you make it there without the engine overheating? Will the brakes decide today's the day they retire? It's like playing Russian roulette with your schedule and your safety.

The High Cost of Outdated Features

Modern cars come with a cornucopia of safety features. Airbags, ABS, traction control, and backup cameras are all there to make driving safe and easy. Your $3,000 special? I hope it has seatbelts.

Skimping on safety features is like trying to save money on a parachute. Sure, you might never need it, but if you do, you'll really wish you had sprung for the good one.

The Fuel Economy Fallacy

Remember when gas was cheap? Are you thinking back to your childhood? Older cars are notorious gas guzzlers. That $3,000 price tag starts to look a lot less attractive when you're stopping at the pump a lot.

The Depreciation Depression

Here's a fun fact: that $3,000 car? It's going to be worth $2,000 next year—and $1,000 the year after that (if you're lucky). Eventually, you'll be paying someone to take it off your hands.

Depreciation on a cheap car is like watching ice cream melt on a hot sidewalk. It happens fast, it's messy, and in the end, you're left with nothing but regret.

The Hidden Costs of "Saving Money"

When you buy a $3,000 car, you're not just buying a vehicle. You're buying:

1. **Stress**: Will it start today?
2. **Time**: Hours spent waiting for tows and at repair shops.
3. **Inconvenience**: Missing work, appointments, or events due to breakdowns.
4. **Risk**: Potentially compromising your safety with outdated features.
5. **Inefficiency**: Spending more on gas than you would with a more modern vehicle.

All these factors have real costs, both financial and personal, that far outweigh the initial "savings" of buying cheap.

Alternatives to Consider

While a $3,000 car might seem like a great deal, there are other options to consider that might be more financially sound in the long run:

1. Saving up for a slightly more expensive but more reliable used car.
2. Looking into certified pre-owned vehicles with warranties.
3. Exploring financing options for newer used cars.
4. Consider leasing as an option for driving a newer, more reliable vehicle.

Rethinking Cheap Car Purchases

Look, I understand it. I've done it myself. Buying a cheap car feels like you're gaming the system. I've bought a $3,000 car before. Only to find out it needed major suspension repairs ($3,000) and eventually a head gasket ($6,000).

The next time you're tempted by that $3,000 "deal," take a moment. Consider the true cost of ownership. Factor in the repairs, the fuel inefficiency, the lack of modern features, the stress, and the potential safety issues. Then, look at your other options.

Remember, in the world of cars, sometimes you have to spend money to save money. The cheapest option upfront isn't always the most economical in the long run. Smart financial decisions aren't just about spending less today; they're about making choices that benefit you in the long term. And when it comes to cars, that often means steering clear of the $3,000 "bargain."

15

Lease A Car

Debunking the "Buy, Don't Lease" Mantra

Let's start with a confession: I used to be one of those financial gurus who'd preach that "leasing is fleecing." I'd wax poetic about depreciation, equity, and the virtues of driving a car until the wheels fell off. But here's the thing: I was wrong.

The truth is, the old "never lease a car" advice is about as practical as one-handed applause. It's time to shift gears and take a fresh look at why leasing might just be a wise financial move.

Why "Buy a Beater" is Bogus Advice

Here's a scenario for you: You're living paycheck to paycheck, your bank account constantly flirts with zero every month, and some financial expert in their ivory tower tells you to just "buy a cheap $3,000 car."

Excuse me? If you had $3,000 lying around, you wouldn't be in this mess in the first place. And, of course, we've already covered the amazing gems you get for $3,000.

This is where leasing shines. Instead of draining your non-existent savings, you can snag a reliable ride for as little as $99 to $199 a month.

Why Your Jalopy is Jeopardizing Your Job

Let's get real for a second. Your car isn't just a way to get from A to B. It's your ticket to keeping your job, which, last time I checked, is pretty important for that whole "having money" thing.

A leased car is usually new, which means it's reliable. No surprise transmission failures, no mysterious knocking sounds, no praying to the automotive gods every time you turn the key. It's peace of mind on four wheels.

Think about it. What's the cost of missing a day of work because your bargain-bin beater decided to take an unscheduled vacation? Suddenly, that cheap car is looking pretty expensive.

The Cash Flow Champion

With leasing, you're looking at predictable, manageable monthly payments. No saving up for a down payment, no unexpected repair bills, just a fixed cost you can budget for.

And if you play your cards right (more on that later), you might even snag a deal that makes your monthly payment lower than your phone bill.

How to Lease Like a Boss

Now, let's talk strategy. Leasing isn't just about walking into a dealership and taking whatever they offer. It's about being smarter than the system.

Here's a pro tip. Look for the ugly ducklings. That car in the weird color that's been sitting on the lot for months? The model that looks like it was designed by a committee of blindfolded actuaries instead of artists? If there are models that everyone hates, those are your golden tickets.

Dealerships are desperate to move these cars, which means you can often lease them for a song. I'm talking about nothing down, $99 a month kind of deals. I've done this twice when I was earning a paycheck but didn't have any cash. I leased a Jeep Liberty with zero down and $99/month. I leased a GMC

Terrain with zero down and $199/month. Both of these cars had something in common. They weren't very popular, so lease deals were plentiful. However, they were a lot nicer than any car I could've afforded at that time. No, you might not be driving your dream car, but you'll be driving – and that's what matters.

How Your Car Affects Your Career

Let's talk about something the financial gurus often miss: the connection between your car and your career.

Your boss doesn't care about your brilliant financial strategy of driving a rust bucket held together by duct tape and prayers. They care about you showing up on time, looking presentable, and not asking for advances because your car broke down again. Your boss will probably be sympathetic the first time you have a car breakdown. But by the second, you might be on the shortlist for replacement.

A leased car gives you reliability and a professional image. It tells your employer, "I've got my act together." And in the world of work, perception often becomes reality.

Why Leasing Beats Long-Term Commitment

Life changes fast. That perfect car you bought might not be so perfect in three years when you've got two kids and a dog.

Leasing gives you flexibility. Don't like the car? In one or two years, you can switch it up. Job situation changed? You're not stuck with a long-term loan. It's like dating instead of getting married – you get to test drive different lifestyles without the long-term commitment.

Leasing as a Lifeline

Look, I'm not saying leasing is for everyone. If you're rolling in dough and can pay cash for a new car every few years, knock yourself out. But for many of us living in the real world, leasing isn't just a good option – it might be the only sensible option.

It's about matching your transportation strategy to your financial reality. It's about reliability, predictability, and giving yourself the breathing room to focus on building your financial future instead of worrying about whether your car will start tomorrow morning.

So the next time some financial guru tries to shame you for considering a lease, remember this: The smartest financial move is the one that works for your life, not theirs. And for many of us, that move just might be leasing. The goal isn't to own a car. The goal is to build a life. And sometimes, the best way to do that is to lease your ride and own your future.

V

Saving

Saving for a rainy day sounds prudent, but is it really the best use of your money? Let's challenge traditional savings advice and explore alternative approaches to building financial security. Your piggy bank is about to get a makeover.

16

Don't Save For Emergencies

The Sacred Cow of Personal Finance

Ah, the emergency fund. It's the golden child of personal finance advice, right up there with "don't spend more than you earn" and "only invest in index funds." But what if I told you that, in some cases, religiously setting aside money for emergencies is making your situation worse?

Now, before you start furiously typing that strongly worded email, let's discuss the math and the reality. I'm not saying emergency funds are useless. But I am saying that sometimes it shouldn't be your priority.

When Your Safety Net Becomes a Noose

Let's imagine you're juggling credit card debt growing faster than you want to admit. The interest rates are so high you wonder if they're legal. And yet, there you are, dutifully squirreling away $50 a month into your emergency fund because that's what you're supposed to do, right?

Wrong.

In this scenario, your well-intentioned emergency fund is actually working against you. It's like trying to bail out a sinking ship with a teaspoon while ignoring the gaping hole in the hull. Sure, you've got a little cash set aside, but your debt is ballooning out of control.

The Math Doesn't Lie

Let's break it down with some very basic numbers:

Say you've got $5,000 in credit card debt at 29% APR. You're paying $130/month towards your credit card. You're also trying to build an emergency fund, setting aside $80 a month.

After a year:

- Your emergency fund: $960 (Yay?)
- Your remaining debt: $4,874 (Wait, what?)

If you paid that extra $80/month towards your credit card, you wouldn't have an emergency fund yet, but your credit card balance would be $3,776. You'd avoid an extra $100 in interest charges.

But that's only half the story. By directing the full $210/month towards your credit card, you'd pay it off completely after 36 months. But if you kept saving $80/month and paid only $130/month towards the balance, it would take 112 months to pay it off. That's over six additional years!

The Emergency Fund in Disguise

Here's a mind-bender for you. If you're carrying high-interest debt, your credit card is already your emergency fund.

I know. Using credit cards for emergencies sounds about as responsible as using a flamethrower to light birthday candles. But stick with me here.

If you have $1,000 in cash and $1,000 in high-interest debt, the debt cancels out the cash, and you're left with nothing... except more interest piling up each month. If you pay the cash towards the debt, you still have nothing, but you're also not incurring new interest charges.

If a $1,000 emergency pops up, in the first scenario, you'll pay it with cash and be left with $1,000 in credit card debt. In the second scenario, you'd charge the emergency to the credit card and still have $1,000 of credit card debt.

By focusing all your extra cash on paying down your debt instead of building an emergency fund, you're actually giving yourself more financial flexibility. Every dollar you pay off is a dollar you can borrow again if (and only if) a real emergency crops up.

But What About Job Loss?

"But Peter," I hear you cry, "what if I lose my job? Shouldn't I have cash saved up?"

First off, if you think a job loss is on the horizon, it's time to switch to financial survival mode. That means throwing every spare penny at your debt regardless of the math.

Why? Because if the worst happens and you do lose your job:

1. You'll have less debt hanging over your head.
2. You'll have more available credit to fall back on if needed.
3. You can still use credit cards for many expenses while unemployed.
4. Unemployment benefits may cover the essentials that can't be charged.

Yes, you might end up accumulating more debt during unemployment. But you'd be in the same boat (or worse) if you'd been holding onto cash instead of paying down debt, thanks to those aggressive interest charges.

When It's Actually Okay to Save for Emergencies

Now, I'm not a complete emergency fund contrarian. If you're debt-free and your finances are in balance, then by all means, build that emergency fund. Heck, make it rain emergency funds!

But if you're drowning in high-interest debt, it's time to rethink your priorities. Your emergency fund isn't just sitting there looking pretty – it's actively costing you money.

Think Critically, Act Boldly

Personal finance isn't about blindly following rules. It's about understanding the principles behind those rules and applying them intelligently to your unique situation.

So the next time you're tempted to set aside that cash for your emergency fund while your credit card debt grows like a weed in a rainstorm, think about whether you're really preparing for emergencies or just drawing out your debt.

17

Only Save $2,500 For Emergencies

Debunking Financial Urban Legends

Let's start with another controversial statement: you're probably saving too much for emergencies. Now, before you accuse me of simply repeating the previous chapter, let me explain that I want to talk about emergency funds once you're ready for one. First, I have to address the infamous "$400 emergency" statistic. You've probably heard that half of Americans would be ruined by an unexpected $400 expense. It's quoted so often that it's practically financial gospel.

But it's not true. At least, not in the way it's typically presented.

The actual study asked people how they'd handle an unexpected $400 expense. Nearly two-thirds of the respondents said they would pay for it entirely with cash or equivalents. Of the remainder that said they could not fully cover it, many said they'd pay for most of it and then put the rest on a credit card or borrow from family and pay it off the following month. That's a far cry from financial ruin. It's like claiming people are on the brink of starvation because they'd need to grocery shop if an unexpected guest came for dinner.

When Financial Advice Defies Gravity

Now, let's talk about the wildly inconsistent savings advice out there. First, you're told to save $500. Then $1,000. And then, suddenly, you're expected to have three to six months of expenses tucked away.

It's like a never-ending staircase designed by M.C. Escher. The first few steps are a gentle climb, and then bam! You're scaling a financial Everest. For someone spending $100,000 a year, that could mean socking away $50,000 in cash. That's not an emergency fund; that's a "buy a second home" fund.

What the Numbers Really Say

Here's where it gets interesting. When you dig into the actual research (yes, I did that so you don't have to), you'll find that most studies suggest a much more reasonable emergency fund: between $2,500 and $3,000.

This isn't just a number pulled out of thin air. It's based on real data about the kinds of emergencies people actually face. Car repairs, appliance replacements, unexpected bills - the vast majority of these fall within this range.

In fact, having $2,500 to $3,000 saved could cover up to 98% of all the financial emergencies a typical family might encounter within a year. It's like buying a backup generator to handle power outages at your home instead of building an entire power plant.

When Saving Becomes Possible, Not Paralyzing

Here's the beauty of this $2,500 target. It's actually achievable for most people. Telling someone living paycheck to paycheck to save six months of expenses is like telling them to flap their arms and fly to the moon. It's not just unhelpful; it's demoralizing.

But $2,500? That's a number people can wrap their heads around. It's a goal that feels possible, not paralyzing. And let's be real: having $2,500 in the bank feels a whole lot better than having nothing, even if it's not the

Rolls-Royce of savings accounts some experts recommend.

Building Your Safety Net

So, how do you get to this magic $2,500 number? It's simple: you start small and stay consistent. Set up an automatic transfer of $50 or $100 from each paycheck into a separate savings account. Before you know it, you'll be halfway there.

And here's a pro tip: don't touch this money unless it's a true emergency. A sale at your favorite store is not an emergency. Your cousin's destination wedding is not an emergency. A zombie apocalypse? That definitely qualifies.

Why $2,500 is the New $50,000

Here's the real kicker: having $2,500 saved can give you almost as much peace of mind as having $50,000 saved without the stress of trying to amass a small fortune.

Think about it. Most of life's little (and not so little) emergencies fall within this range. Car repairs, medical deductibles, unexpected travel - all of these become manageable speed bumps rather than life-altering catastrophes when you've got $2,500 in the bank.

Adapting to Your Financial Reality

Now, I'm not saying $2,500 is a magic number for everyone. If you're earning seven figures, by all means, save more. If you've got a fleet of unreliable classic cars or a small zoo in your backyard, you might want to bump that number up (see Netflix's *Tiger King*).

The point is to have a realistic, achievable target based on your actual life, not some arbitrary rule of thumb that doesn't account for individual circumstances.

Simplify, Save, Succeed

Here's the deal: personal finance doesn't have to be complicated. You don't need a Ph.D. in economics to build a solid financial foundation. What you need is a clear, achievable objective and the discipline to work towards it.

So, forget about the intimidating, often unrealistic savings targets you've heard before. Focus on building that $2,500 emergency fund. Once you've hit that target, sure, keep saving if you can. But don't stress if you can't immediately sock away half a year's salary.

Remember, the best emergency fund is the one you actually have, not the one you're endlessly chasing. So start small, stay consistent, and give yourself a pat on the back when you hit that $2,500 mark. You're not just saving money; you're buying peace of mind.

18

Don't Save In A Savings Account

The "Savings" Misnomer

We talked about savings. Now, let's talk about savings accounts. You know, those financial products that banks tout as the perfect home for your hard-earned cash. The ones with interest rates so low, you'd need a microscope to see the growth. Yeah, those.

Here's a shocking revelation: despite what the name suggests, a savings account might be the worst place to keep your savings. It's like finding out that the tooth fairy is actually your dad. But stick with me here because this financial enlightenment could be the difference between retiring and retiring happy.

The $100 Savings Account Strategy

If you peeked into my online banking right now, you'd see less than $100 in my savings account. No, I haven't blown all my money on Star Trek memorabilia yet (but you should see my collection of vintage cellular phones). I've just found better places for it to hang out and actually grow.

Keeping large sums in a savings account is like trying to grow a garden in the Sahara. Sure, it's technically possible, but why make life so hard for yourself?

Your Savings Account on Steroids

Now, let me introduce you to the Roth IRA – the superhero of the savings world. It's like a savings account, but instead of giving you pennies in interest, it has the potential to rain dollar bills.

Here's the Roth IRA in a nutshell:

- You contribute after-tax money (Uncle Sam's already taken his cut)
- Your investments grow tax-deferred (no taxes on those gains, baby!)
- When you withdraw in retirement, it's all tax-free (take that, future tax rates!)

But here's the kicker – you can withdraw your contributions at any time without paying taxes or penalties. It's like having your cake and eating it and then being told the cake was calorie-free.

The Emergency Fund Paradox

Now, I can hear you asking, "But what about emergencies? Isn't that what savings accounts are for?" Well, let's think about this logically for a second.

How often do you actually have a financial emergency? If you're having them frequently, we need to have a different conversation about insurance and lifestyle choices. But for most of us, true financial emergencies are about as common as a polite political debate.

In my 25 years of working, I've been laid off twice. If I had followed the traditional advice and saved the recommended amount for unemployment all those years, I'd have been squirreling away money for a quarter-century to use it for just a few months. That's like preparing for a week-long camping trip by stockpiling 25 years' worth of baked beans. It just doesn't make sense.

Your Financial Swiss Army Knife

So, here's where the Roth IRA shines. It's not just a retirement account; it's a financial Swiss Army knife. Need some emergency cash? Withdraw your contributions. The market's booming, and you don't need the money? Let it ride and watch it grow. It's the best of both worlds – the accessibility of a savings account with the growth potential of an investment account.

Let's break it down:

1. Contribute to your Roth IRA regularly (up to the annual limit).
2. Invest in a mix of stocks, bonds, or whatever floats your financial boat (and your professional investment advisor recommends).
3. If an emergency hits, withdraw what you need from your contributions.
4. If you don't need it, let it grow and compound over time.

It's like planting a money tree that you can occasionally pluck a few leaves from without killing it.

The Time is Now

Here's the thing about Roth IRAs – they come with income limits. As your career progresses and your income grows, you might find yourself ineligible to contribute. That's why starting early is key. It's like getting into an exclusive club before you're too old and lame to be allowed in.

So, stop treating your savings account like it's doing you any favors. It's time to break up with that low-interest sloth and start a passionate affair with a Roth IRA. Your future self will thank you – probably from the first-class cabin of your flight to Tahiti.

Think Smart, Save Smarter

Look, I'm not saying to close your savings account entirely. Keep a little cash there for immediate needs. But for your real savings? The money that's meant to grow and be there on the off-chance you really need it? Give it the home it deserves in a Roth IRA.

Remember, in the world of personal finance, conventional wisdom isn't always wise. Sometimes, the smartest move is to zig when everyone else zags. And in this case, that zig might just be the difference between financial mediocrity and financial mastery.

19

Don't Save For College

Unpacking the College Savings Pressure

Let's talk about that nagging voice in your head. It starts whispering the moment your bundle of joy arrives: "Start saving for college now, or you're a terrible parent!"

It's so frightening that you rush out and open a 529 plan, throw a few bucks into it, and then breathe a sigh of relief. But what if I told you that voice isn't just annoying – it might be steering you towards financial disaster?

It's time to rip off the band-aid: saving for your child's college education might be one of the worst financial moves you can make. Yes, you read that right. Let's dive into why your kid's 529 plan might be the Trojan horse in your financial fortress.

Your Golden Years Come First

Here's a hard truth: many people won't be able to retire, no matter what they do now. So why on earth would you siphon precious dollars away from your retirement fund to pay for your kid's education?

Think of it this way: every dollar you squirrel away for college is a dollar that's not compounding in your retirement account. It's like robbing your certain future to pay for a maybe. And let's face it, your future self is going to need that money a lot more than your kid needs a debt-free diploma.

How Savings Can Backfire

Now, here's where it gets really interesting. That college fund you've been dutifully filling? It might actually be working against your child when it comes to financial aid.

The Free Application for Federal Student Aid (FAFSA) looks at your family's financial picture to determine aid. And guess what? That 529 plan counts as an asset. So, congratulations! Your diligent saving might have just reduced the amount of aid your child can receive.

Meanwhile, certain assets are excluded from FAFSA calculations. Retirement accounts, annuities, and your home equity don't count. So, if you really want to give your kid a leg up on financial aid, you might be better off pumping up your 401(k) or paying down your mortgage.

Debunking the Savings-Options Link

Now, I can hear you protesting: "But if I don't save, my precious prodigy won't be able to go to their dream school!" Well, I'm about to flip that notion on its head.

The Elite College Aid Bonanza

Here's a juicy secret the college savings industry doesn't want you to know: Those eye-popping, expensive elite colleges? They're often the ones throwing money at students. Why? Because they're sitting on endowments that would make a billionaire blush.

Take Harvard and Princeton, for example. If your family makes less than $75,000 a year, your kid could attend for free. Yes, you read that right. Free. And they're not alone. Many top-tier schools have similar policies. So, while you're scrimping and saving to afford State U, little Timmy might actually have a better shot at a full ride to an Ivy.

The Net Price Reality Check

"But what about those terrifying sticker prices?" I hear you. Well, here's where it gets interesting. Thanks to a little thing called the Net Price Calculator (which every college is required to have), you can get a pretty good estimate of what you'll actually pay before your kid even applies.

And, surprise, that swanky private college might end up costing you less out of pocket than the state school down the road. Why? Because they have more money to play with when it comes to financial aid.

The FAFSA Flat-Rate Phenomenon

Now, let's talk more about FAFSA, which is the form that determines your Student Aid Index (SAI) or what was previously called your Expected Family Contribution (EFC). Here's the kicker: Your family contribution doesn't particularly change if your kid is eyeing Community College or Yale. It's based on your family's financial situation, not the cost of the school.

So whether your kid is looking at a $20,000-a-year state school or a $70,000-a-year private college, FAFSA says you can afford to kick in the same amount. The more expensive school? They're on the hook to make up the difference if they want your kid badly enough.

There's Always a Way

Here's something the college savings industrial complex doesn't want you to know: your kids can get through college without your help. Shocking, I know.

Take my alma mater, Northwestern University, for example. Like many well-endowed schools, they guarantee that students won't have to take on loans if their families can't afford to pay. That's right – if you can't pay, they'll cover it.

And even for schools without such generous policies, there's almost always a path. Grants, scholarships, work-study, loans – the options are there. Will your kid graduate debt-free? Maybe not. But they'll graduate. And isn't that the point?

Keeping Your Options Open

Let's say you do manage to save a chunk of change for college. Great! But what if your kid decides college isn't for them? What if they go to trade school? What if they join the military? Or what if they get a full-ride scholarship? Suddenly, that 529 plan isn't looking so smart.

By keeping your money in more flexible accounts – like your retirement funds or home equity – you're giving yourself options. If you end up in a position to help with college costs, great! If not, you haven't sacrificed your financial security.

Securing Your Own Oxygen Mask First

Remember those pre-flight safety demonstrations? "Secure your own oxygen mask before assisting others." The same principle applies to your finances.

By focusing on your own financial security first, you're actually setting your kids up for long-term success. Think about it. Would you rather have your kids graduate with some student loan debt or have them support you financially in your golden years because you can't afford to retire?

Rethinking College Savings

Look, I'm not saying you should never help your kids with college if you can afford it. But before you start funneling money into that 529 plan, ask yourself:

- Am I on track for retirement?

- Have I maximized my tax-advantaged retirement accounts?
- Do I have a solid emergency fund?
- Have I paid off high-interest debt?

If the answer to any of these is "no," then you have no business saving for your kid's college education.

Instead, focus on securing your own financial future. Max out those retirement accounts. Pay down that mortgage. Build that emergency fund. Not only will this put you in a better position to help your kids if you choose to down the line, but it might actually improve their chances of getting financial aid.

Remember, there are loans for college, but there are no loans for retirement. Your kids have their whole lives ahead of them to build wealth and pay off debt. You, on the other hand, are on a much tighter timeline.

So the next time that guilty voice pipes up about college savings, dismiss it. Your financial security takes priority. And your kids? They'll figure it out. After all, isn't learning to solve problems and overcome challenges what college is all about?

And who knows? You might just be giving them an incredible gift by not saving for their college. They might attend a dream school they never thought possible, all thanks to the counterintuitive logic of financial aid. Now, that's what I call getting educated.

20

Don't Set Financial Goals

How Ambition Can Be Your Worst Enemy

Let's start with a confession: I used to be a goal-setting junkie. Vision boards, SMART objectives, five-year plans - you name it, I did it. And you know what? It was about as effective as trying to nail jello to a wall.

Before you accuse me of going soft or lacking ambition, check this out. Goals aren't inherently bad. But they're like sugar - a little bit can give you energy, but too much can rot your teeth and give you diabetes.

The problem with goals is that they create artificial finish lines in a race that never really ends. They trick you into thinking you're done once you cross that line. Mission accomplished. But life doesn't work that way.

How Goals Box You In

Here's a mind-bender for you: goals can actually limit your potential. Sounds counterintuitive, right? But think about it. When you set a specific goal, you're essentially putting blinders on yourself. You're saying, "This is the endpoint, and anything beyond it doesn't matter."

But what if your true potential lies beyond that arbitrary endpoint? What if you're capable of so much more but stop pushing because you've hit your target?

It's like telling Bryson DeChambeau, "Your goal is to shoot under par." He'd hit that goal and stop, never knowing he could card a 58.

When Achievement Feels Empty

Let's talk about the dirty little secret of goal-setting: achieving your goals can be incredibly anticlimactic. You bust your butt for months or years to reach this arbitrary milestone, and when you finally get there... yawn.

It's like climbing a mountain, only to realize the view isn't as spectacular as you imagined. And now what? You're standing on top of a mountain with nowhere else to go.

But when you focus on the process - the daily climb, the skills you're building, the person you're becoming - every day becomes its own reward. You're not waiting for some future moment to feel fulfilled; you're finding fulfillment in the here and now.

Small Actions, Big Results

Here's where it gets really interesting. When you ditch the big, hairy, audacious goals and focus instead on small, consistent actions, something magical happens. You tap into the power of compound growth.

It's the difference between trying to fill a swimming pool with a fire hose and a steady drip. The fire hose might seem more impressive, but it's exhausting and will wear you out. On the other hand, the steady drip will eventually fill that pool - and you'll never even notice it.

Take my YouTube channel, for example. If I had set a goal of "100 million views and $1 million in revenue," I probably would have quit before I even started. It would have seemed impossible, especially when my videos struggled to reach five views. Instead, I just focused on creating content consistently. Before I knew it, I had posted 7,000 videos, hired a team, and, yes, blew right through those seemingly impossible milestones.

Finding Freedom in Process

Goals come with baggage. They create pressure, stress, and anxiety. If you miss a milestone, you suddenly feel like a failure. But when you focus on the process, that pressure evaporates.

It's like the difference between staring at the top of Mount Everest and freaking out versus just focusing on taking the next step in front of you. One approach paralyzes you with fear; the other keeps you moving forward.

By focusing on habits and small actions, you free yourself from the tyranny of outcomes. You're no longer a success or failure based on whether you hit some arbitrary target. You're succeeding every day simply by showing up and doing the work.

Adapting in a Changing World

Another problem with rigid goals is that they don't play well with our rapidly changing world. Set a five-year plan, and I guarantee the world will throw you a curveball before you're even halfway there.

But when you focus on processes and habits, you're building adaptable skills and mindsets. You're not locked into a specific outcome; you're prepared for whatever opportunities come your way.

It's like the difference between memorizing answers for a test versus actually understanding the subject. One approach falls apart as soon as you face an unexpected question; the other allows you to tackle any problem that comes your way.

Building Your Road to Success

So if not goals, then what? Simple: small integrated processes. Think about the simple, repeatable actions you can integrate into your daily life. These are the true building blocks of success.

Think about it like this: Would you rather try to run a marathon tomorrow or walk one mile every day for a year? The marathon might seem more impressive, but the daily walk will take you much further in the long run (pun intended).

This approach has been a game-changer for me. Those dozen books I've published? They didn't come from a goal to become a prolific author. They came from a simple habit of jotting down ideas whenever they came to me. Before I knew it, I had enough material for multiple books.

How does this apply to your finances? Instead of having a savings goal, just have a process of continuously saving. Instead of focusing on saving $1,000 in an emergency fund, intentionally save whatever you can whenever you can.

Now, let's talk about that magic number your financial advisor keeps throwing at you. That overwhelming sum they say you need to retire without having to subsist on ramen noodles and leftover cat food. Instead of obsessing over hitting some arbitrary savings goal, why not try the same thing? Just save.

Think of saving like you're a work in progress. You're not aiming for a specific target; you're honing your skills, always looking for opportunities to strike. See an extra $5 in your pocket? Throw that into your savings account. Got a raise? Congratulations. Now, direct that to your retirement fund.

The beauty of this approach? The act of saving becomes the achievement. You might wake up one day and realize you've hit your emergency fund goal without even trying. Or you'll check your retirement account and find out you're way ahead of schedule.

And the best part? Once you've built this savings habit, it becomes as natural as breathing. You'll be blowing past those arbitrary goals because it's just a part of your routine.

Moving Forward Without a Map

The beautiful thing about focusing on progress rather than goals is that you don't need to have it all figured out. You don't need a detailed roadmap or a clear destination. You just need to keep moving forward.

It's like being an explorer in uncharted territory. You don't know exactly what you'll find, but every step forward is a discovery. And often, the discoveries you make along the way are far more valuable than any predetermined destination could have been.

Action Trumps Planning

Look, I get it. Ditching goals can feel scary. We've been conditioned to believe that without clear objectives, we're just wandering aimlessly. But I'm here to tell you that your work is infinitely more valuable than the planning you perfect.

So here's your new action plan (ironic, I know):

1. Stop setting goals.
2. Identify small, repeatable actions that move you in a general direction you find appealing.
3. Focus on showing up every day and performing those actions, regardless of how you feel.
4. Stay open to opportunities and adjust your course as you go.
5. Celebrate your progress, no matter how small it seems.

Remember, life isn't a race to a finish line. It's a journey of continuous growth and discovery. By focusing on the process rather than the outcome, you open yourself up to possibilities you never could have imagined.

So go ahead and tear up that goal list. Stop trying to plan every detail of your future. Instead, start taking small, consistent actions today. After all, the best way to predict the future is to create it – one small step at a time.

VI

Credit

Credit isn't the boogeyman it's often made out to be. Let's explore how strategic use of credit can actually enhance your financial position. It's time to make credit work for you, not against you.

21

There Is No Good Or Bad Debt

The Good, the Bad, and the Ugly Truth About Debt

Let's start by mixing things up right away: there's no such thing as "good debt" or "bad debt." For years, we've been fed this line that some debts are virtuous (hello, mortgages and student loans) while others are the financial equivalent of burning a pile of cash (credit card debt). But it's time to pull back the curtain on this grand illusion.

When "Good" Goes Bad

Remember the housing bubble of 2008? So do millions of homeowners who suddenly found their "good debt" turning into a financial nightmare faster than you can say "subprime mortgage."

The truth is, there are no guarantees in the world of debt. That house you bought might not appreciate. That business you invested in might go belly-up. That degree you're still paying for might not lead to the high-paying job you were promised.

"Good debt" can go bad faster than milk left out on a hot summer day. And when it does, it doesn't care about the label we've slapped on it.

Finding Gold in Unexpected Places

Now, let's flip the script. What about that "bad debt" we've been taught to avoid, like the plague? The vacation you financed and the car you bought on credit are supposed to be financial sins.

Not so fast. Sometimes, that "frivolous" vacation is exactly what you need to avoid burnout and return to work recharged and ready to earn that promotion. That car might be the reliable transportation you need to keep earning that paycheck or get to a better-paying job across town.

The point is that context matters. Debt isn't inherently good or bad - it's how you use it that counts.

Stop Blaming, Start Planning

Here's where it gets really interesting. This whole "good debt/bad debt" narrative is often used to deflect responsibility.

"It's not my fault I'm underwater on my mortgage - it was supposed to be good debt!"

"I know this credit card debt is bad, so I guess I'm just bad with money."

Both of these statements miss the point entirely. Debt is a tool, like a chainsaw. Used carefully, it can help you build great things. If used carelessly, well... you end up in the emergency room. But which time was it the chainsaw's fault?

Understanding the True Cost of Debt

Here's the thing about debt that the "good debt/bad debt" crowd often misses: it's all about risk and reward. Every time you take on debt, you're making a bet. Sometimes, it pays off big time; sometimes, it doesn't.

The key is to understand the risks, have a solid plan, and be prepared for things not to go according to that plan. Because let's face it, life has a funny way of throwing curveballs when we least expect them.

Using Debt to Get in the Game

One of the most powerful aspects of debt is its ability to get you into games you otherwise couldn't play. Want to invest in real estate but don't have a couple hundred grand lying around? Debt can get you there. Want to start a business but don't have the capital? A loan might be your ticket.

Debt is like a financial time machine. It allows you to bring future earnings into the present, giving you opportunities now that you'd otherwise have to wait years or decades for.

Rethinking Your Relationship with Debt

So, where does this leave us? Should we all run out and max out our credit cards in the name of opportunity? No. But we should rethink our relationship with debt.

Instead of asking, "Is this good debt or bad debt?" try asking:

- Do I have a solid plan for using this debt?
- What's the potential upside?
- What's the worst-case scenario, and can I handle it?
- How does this fit into my overall financial strategy?

Not a Moral Judgment

At the end of the day, debt is just a financial tool. It's not good or bad, virtuous or sinful. It's simply a way to leverage current opportunities against future earnings.

If used wisely, it can be rocket fuel that propels you to financial success. Used carelessly, it can be the anchor that drags you down. The difference isn't in the type of debt - it's in how you use it.

So the next time someone starts preaching about good debt and bad debt, feel free to smile and nod. But remember, in the world of finance, things are rarely black and white. It's all shades of gray and, hopefully, eventually green.

    Your job isn't to avoid "bad" debt or only take on "good" debt. It's to use debt strategically, responsibly, and aligned with your financial goals. Because at the end of the day, the only truly good debt is the kind that moves you closer to where you want to be.

22

Get As Much Credit As You Can

When Debt Becomes Your Best Friend

Let's start with a statement that will make just about everyone cringe: you should be actively seeking as much credit as you can get. While conventional wisdom tells us to avoid debt like the plague, I'm here to tell you that credit, when wielded correctly, can be your secret weapon in the quest for financial freedom.

Now, before you dismiss this, let's cover some details. I'm not talking about maxing out your credit cards on frivolous purchases. While I am talking about getting as much credit as possible, I'm also not trying to create a massive temptation for you. I'm talking about strategically positioning yourself to take advantage of opportunities that only come to those with access to capital.

Credit as Your Emergency Responder

Here's the obvious scenario. It's 3 AM, and you wake up to the sound of water gushing from a burst pipe. Your emergency fund? It's tied up in a high-yield savings account that takes days to access. But your credit card? It's ready to get the work started right now.

Having access to a high credit limit is like having a financial firefighter on standby 24/7. It's there when you need it, no questions asked. And the best part? If you don't need it, it costs you nothing.

And I'm not talking about just getting more credit cards (although that can work). I'm talking about lines of credit (personal or business). Like a credit card, there's no cost until you use them. But unlike a credit card that pays a vendor directly, lines of credit make cash available directly to you for purchases that might otherwise not be possible. With a line of credit, you could buy a car from a private seller or a vacation home from an estate. Try that with a credit card.

Seizing Moments with Monetary Muscle

Here's a truth bomb for you: some of the best opportunities in life come with a price tag attached. Whether it's a chance to invest in a promising startup, snag a rental property at a bargain price, or take advantage of a once-in-a-lifetime business opportunity, having access to credit can be the difference between seizing the moment and watching it slip away.

Remember, the wealthy don't just save money - they leverage it. And credit is one of the most powerful leverage tools at your disposal.

Growing Your Financial Garden

Contrary to popular belief, having high credit limits can actually boost your credit score. It's all about that magical thing called credit utilization ratio. The more credit you have available and don't use, the better you look to lenders.

It's like having a massive garden but cultivating only a small plot. Lenders see all that unused space and think, "Wow, this person has so much potential, and they're not even using it all. They must be super responsible!"

Playing Hardball with Lenders

Here's a little secret the banks don't want you to know: the more credit you have access to, the more power you have to negotiate better terms. It's simple supply and demand. If you have multiple credit lines with high limits, you become a hot commodity. Lenders will trip over themselves to offer you better rates and perks.

It's like being the popular kid in high school, but instead of getting invited to all the parties, you're getting invited to constantly lower interest rates.

Smoothing Out Life's Financial Turbulence

For entrepreneurs and small business owners, access to credit can be the difference between smooth sailing and capsizing when cash flow gets choppy. It's not about living beyond your means; it's about bridging the gap between invoices and payroll or investing in growth opportunities that will pay off down the line. Take my friend, Bob, for example. He owns a business that stamps automotive products. One day, a competitor closed their doors, but they had a million-dollar machine he wanted. They told him that he could have it if he could pay them $200,000 today. Otherwise, it would go to auction and easily command $800,000. Thanks to his extensive credit line, he wired them the money within a couple of hours and doubled his production capacity.

Why Timing Is Everything

Here's a nugget of wisdom that could save your financial bacon one day: the best time to build credit is when you don't need it. Banks are funny that way - they're most willing to throw money at you when you're least desperate for it.

So, even if you're sitting pretty right now, with a stable job and a healthy savings account, that's precisely when you should be applying for credit limit increases or new lines of credit. It's like stocking up on umbrellas on a sunny day - it might seem silly now, but you'll be glad you did when the storm hits.

Credit as Your Financial Superpower

Look, I get it. The idea of actively seeking more credit goes against everything we've been taught about responsible financial management. But here's the thing: the old rules were written for a world that no longer exists.

In today's fast-paced, opportunity-rich environment, credit isn't just a safety net - it's a launching pad. It's the difference between playing defense with your finances and going on the offensive.

So here's your action plan:

1. Apply for credit limit increases on your existing lines.
2. Look for new opportunities that are more accessible or lower cost.
3. Keep your credit utilization low, but don't be afraid to deploy your credit strategically.
4. Always, always, always pay off your balances as quickly as you can.

Remember, credit is a tool. In the right hands, it's not a pathway to ruin - it's a highway to financial freedom. So, if you want to keep yourself in the game of opportunities, get the credit you can.

23

Always Use A Credit Card

Debunking the "Only Spend What You Have" Mantra

We've all heard it before: "Never spend money you don't have." "Cash is king." "Credit cards are evil." "Debit keeps you honest." Well, it's time to toss that advice in the financial trash bin.

Let me tell you a little story that might just change your mind about the "safety" of cash and debit cards. There I was, a responsible adult using my debit card like I was told to. Someone got hold of my card number and drained my entire account faster than you can say "WTF."

Now, you'd think the bank would be all over this. Wrong. Their response? "We'll look into it... but it'll take 60 to 90 days." Meanwhile, I'm left scrounging for dinner money like a college freshman - for months!

That was the day I swore off debit cards for good. And it's just the tip of the iceberg about why credit cards should be your go-to for every purchase.

Your Personal Financial Bodyguard

When it comes to fraud protection, credit cards are the heavyweight champions of the financial world. While debit cards leave you vulnerable, credit cards have your back like a loyal bodyguard.

With a credit card, your liability for unauthorized charges is typically limited to $50 - and many cards offer zero liability. That means if some tech-savvy crook decides to go on a shopping spree with your card number, you're not left holding the bag.

Plus, credit card companies have teams of fraud detectives working around the clock. They're like the CIA of the financial world, spotting suspicious activity faster than you can say "identity theft."

Your Ace in the Hole

Have you ever bought something that turned out to be a dud? With a credit card, you've got an ally in your corner. Credit card companies offer stellar support for resolving disputes with merchants.

Didn't receive that package you ordered? The hotel didn't honor your reservation? No problem. After a quick call to your credit card company, you can often get those charges reversed immediately.

Try doing that with cash or a debit card. You'll be met with shrugs and "Sorry, not our problem."

Getting Paid to Spend

Now, here's where it gets really good. Using a credit card responsibly is like having a personal ATM that spits out rewards instead of fees. We're talking cash back, travel miles, points - the works.

I've personally cashed in tens of thousands of dollars in free rewards. Travel, hotels, gear - you name it. It's like getting paid to shop. And the best part? The credit card companies don't care. For every savvy user like me, they've got thousands of others sending them money faster than they can count it.

Your Ticket to Financial Opportunities

On top of that, every swipe of your credit card is like laying another brick in the foundation of your credit score. And in today's world, a good credit score basically secures your spot in society. It's your ticket to better loan rates, housing opportunities, and sometimes even job prospects.

Using your credit card regularly and responsibly is like sending a monthly letter to the financial world saying, "I'm trustworthy and financially savvy!"

Living the VIP Life

Credit cards aren't just about spending and saving - they're your ticket to the good life. We're talking travel insurance that would make your risk-averse grandma jealous, rental car coverage that'll save you a bundle, and concierge services that make you feel like a celebrity.

Fancy airport lounges? Exclusive discounts? Early access to concert tickets? Your perfect credit card is out there.

Your Financial Safety Net

Life has a funny way of throwing curveballs when you least expect them. The car breaks down? An unexpected medical bill? A sudden need to book a last-minute flight? Your credit card is there, ready to save the day. It may not be the ideal solution, but it's ready to save you from life's little (and big) emergencies.

Savvy Financing at Your Fingertips

Many credit cards offer introductory 0% APR periods on purchases. This is like getting an interest-free loan from your friendly neighborhood bank. Need to make a big purchase but don't have all the cash upfront? Slap it on your zero-interest credit card and pay it off over time without paying a dime in interest.

It's like having a magic wand that turns big, scary purchases into manageable monthly payments.

Credit is King

Look, I get it. Credit cards have gotten a bad rap over the years. But used responsibly, they're not just a convenient way to pay - they're a powerful financial tool that can protect you, reward you, and open doors you never knew existed.

Here's your new financial mantra: Credit for everything, pay it off monthly, reap the rewards.

Remember:

1. Use your credit card for every purchase, no matter how small.
2. Pay your balance in full each month to avoid interest charges.
3. Choose cards with rewards that match your spending habits.
4. Take advantage of all the perks and protections your cards offer.

In the grand chess game of personal finance, your credit card isn't just a pawn - it's the queen, capable of making powerful moves in any direction. Use it wisely, and you'll protect your finances and potentially come out ahead.

24

Ignore Your Credit Score

When Digits Dictate Decisions

I think you should ignore your credit score. I also admit I have churned out more credit score improvement guides, webinars, and courses than I care to admit.

Now, of course, your credit score is important in some ways, but much like your Uber rating or your high school GPA, it has taken on a life of its own. I've seen it become the tail wagging the dog, the puppet master pulling the strings of financial decisions. And frankly, it's time it ends.

When Fear Freezes Progress

Let me tell you a story. I once worked with a client drowning in high-interest debt. We had a golden opportunity to consolidate their loans, slash their interest rates, and set them on a path to financial freedom. The catch? It would ding their credit score by a few points.

Their response? "I can't do it." They chose to keep drowning rather than take a tiny hit to their precious score. It's like refusing to use a life preserver because you're worried it might mess up your hair.

This isn't just silly; it's financially suicidal. A few points on your credit score are nothing compared to the very real dollars you could be saving or the stress you could be alleviating.

When Fear Keeps You Broke

Now, let's talk about the ultimate credit score boogeyman: bankruptcy. I've seen folks who are so deep in debt that they're bailing water with a teaspoon, yet they refuse to consider bankruptcy because – you guessed it – it would tank their credit score.

Here's a reality check. If you're struggling that much with debt, your credit score is probably already on life support. Keeping it artificially inflated while you drain your retirement accounts and sell your kidney on the black market isn't helping anyone, least of all you.

I've worked with countless people who've gone through bankruptcy. Want to know a secret? Many of them now have credit scores over 800. They're financially secure, stress-free, and living their best lives. Meanwhile, the credit score worshippers are still treading water, wondering why they can't get ahead.

When Numbers Trump Living

Here's a sobering thought: You get one life. One shot at this crazy ride we call existence. And you're spending it obsessing over a three-digit number?

I've seen people give up on dreams, miss out on experiences, and live lives of quiet desperation, all in service of maintaining a good credit score. It's like carrying a 4-star rating to the graveyard – congratulations, but what's the point?

Your credit score should be a tool, not your taskmaster. It should work for you, not the other way around. If maintaining a high score is keeping you from living your best life, it's time to reassess your priorities.

When Falling Leads to Flying

Here's the kicker about credit scores: they're resilient little buggers. Yes, taking a big financial step like debt consolidation or bankruptcy might knock your score down in the short term. But guess what? If that step puts you on solid financial footing, your score will bounce back – often higher than before.

It's like setting a broken bone. Yes, it hurts at the moment, and you might be out of commission for a while. But once it heals, you're stronger than ever. Your credit score works the same way. Sometimes, it needs to take a step back to leap forward.

Learning the Hard Way

There's an old saying that experience is the best teacher. When it comes to credit scores, this couldn't be truer. Those who've watched their scores plummet and then rise again often have a much better understanding of how credit really works.

They're not slaves to arbitrary rules or obsessed with gaming the system. They understand the underlying principles and use that knowledge to their advantage. In other words, they've gone from credit score prisoners to credit score masters.

Living for You, Not Your FICO

Look, I'm not saying you should completely ignore your credit score. It's a useful tool in our modern financial world. But it should be just that – a tool, not the blueprint for your entire financial life.

If you're making decisions based primarily on how they'll affect your credit score, it's time to step back and reassess. Ask yourself:

1. Is this decision improving my actual financial situation or just my credit score?

2. Am I giving up important life experiences to maintain my score?
3. Is my obsession with my credit score causing me undue stress or anxiety?
4. Am I avoiding necessary financial steps (like debt consolidation or bankruptcy) because I'm afraid of hurting my score?

If you answered yes to any of these, it might be time to break free from the credit score cult.

Remember, at the end of the day, you're a human being, not a number. Your worth isn't determined by your FICO score, and your life shouldn't be either. Make financial decisions based on what's best for you, your family, and your future – not what's best for that three-digit number.

VII

Family

Families and finances are often a minefield of emotions and expectations. Let's examine unconventional approaches to handling finances that could lead to greater harmony and financial success.

25

Never Merge Your Finances

When "What's Mine is Yours" Goes Wrong

What if combining all your money when you get married is actually a terrible idea? I know it sounds almost sacrilegious. After all, tradition says that marriage is all about becoming "one"?

But here's the thing: while you might share a life, a home, and maybe even a Netflix account, you're still two distinct individuals. And in today's world, where both partners often come into a marriage with established careers, separate bank accounts, and often serious debt, the old "what's mine is yours" approach might be doing more harm than good.

Two Incomes, Two Identities

Gone are the days when one income supported an entire household. Today's couples often marry later, with each partner bringing their own financial history, habits, and baggage to the relationship.

Fully merging finances in this scenario isn't just challenging - it can be downright problematic. It's like trying to merge two different-sized rivers into one stream. Sure, it can be done, but it rarely feels right or fair.

Why Everyone Needs Their Own Money

So, here's what you do. Each partner keeps a portion of their income in a separate account. Let's call it the "Freedom Fund." It's another version of your freedom money. This isn't about secrecy or mistrust. It's about maintaining a sense of financial autonomy and identity within the partnership.

This fund could be used for anything - buying gifts for your spouse (surprise!), indulging in a personal hobby, or even making individual investment decisions. The key is that it's yours to control without needing to consult, explain, or, heaven forbid, ask permission.

Balancing Shared and Separate Finances

Now, I'm not suggesting you keep all your money separate. You could do it, but it might be impractical and potentially divisive. Instead, consider a hybrid approach:

1. **Joint Checking Account**: This is where the bulk of your income goes. It covers shared expenses like mortgage/rent, utilities, groceries, and joint savings goals.
2. **Individual "Freedom Funds"**: Before your paycheck hits the joint account, each partner siphons off a predetermined amount or percentage into their personal account.

This approach gives you the best of both worlds: shared responsibility for household expenses and financial goals, plus individual freedom for personal spending and saving.

Fair Doesn't Always Mean Equal

Here's where it gets interesting. If there's a significant income disparity between partners, consider contributing to shared expenses proportionally based on income.

For example, if Luke earns $100,000 and Lorelai earns $50,000, Luke might contribute 66% to the joint account while Lorelai contributes 33%. This ensures that both partners have an equitable amount left for their personal "Freedom Funds."

Yours, Mine, or Ours?

Now, let's talk about everyone's favorite topic: debt. When one partner brings significant debt into the marriage (student loans and credit cards are the usual suspects), it can be a source of stress and resentment if not handled carefully.

While supporting each other is important, maintaining some financial separation can prevent the debt-free partner from feeling unfairly burdened. It also allows the partner with debt to maintain ownership of their financial situation and work towards resolving it. Their "Freedom Funds" may primarily go towards paying off the debt, leaving both partners with a sense of fairness.

Keeping the Spark Alive

Here's something the "merge everything" crowd often overlooks: the joy of financial surprises in a relationship. When all your money is pooled, it becomes challenging to surprise your partner with gifts or treats without them seeing the transaction.

Maintaining some financial separation allows each partner to plan surprises, whether it's a special date night, a thoughtful gift, a weekend getaway, or an Aston Martin (if you have the means). It keeps an element of excitement and spontaneity in your financial life together.

Fostering Growth and Creativity

Having some financial autonomy isn't just about spending. It's about fostering personal growth and creativity. Maybe you want to take a class to learn a new skill, or perhaps you're interested in starting a side hustle. Having your own money to invest in these pursuits can be incredibly empowering.

This financial freedom can lead to personal development that ultimately benefits the relationship as a whole. After all, a marriage is strongest when both partners are growing, thriving, and content as individuals.

Coordinating Without Combining

While maintaining some financial separation is beneficial, it's crucial to coordinate on long-term goals like retirement. This doesn't mean combining all your retirement accounts but rather ensuring your individual plans align so you can enjoy your golden years together.

Regular check-ins about retirement savings, investment strategies, and timeline goals can help ensure you're on the same page without necessarily being in the same account.

Financial Harmony Through Thoughtful Separation

Some people cringe at combining any finances. For others, the idea of not fully combining finances in marriage might feel counterintuitive. Traditionally, we've been conditioned to think that a complete financial merger is a sign of trust and commitment.

But here's the truth: trust and commitment in a marriage aren't about having one bank account. They're about open communication, shared goals, and mutual respect for each other's individuality - including financial individuality.

By maintaining some financial separation, you're not pulling away from your partner. You're creating a financial structure that respects both your shared life and your individual identities. You're setting the stage for fewer money arguments, more personal fulfillment, and even some financial surprises to keep the spark alive. The strongest marriages aren't built on joint checking accounts. They're built on mutual respect, shared goals, and a little financial freedom.

26

Have Kids Before You Can Afford Them

The Costly Myth of "Being Ready"

You've probably heard and thought, "Wait until you're financially stable to have kids." It's the kind of advice that sounds so sensible, so responsible. But what if I told you that this well-intentioned wisdom might be robbing you of life's greatest adventure?

The truth is if we all waited until we felt 100% financially ready to have kids, the human race would die out. There's never a perfect time to become a parent. But there might be a better time than you think – and it's probably sooner than later.

Needs vs. Wants

Here's a news flash that might shock the baby product industry. Infants don't care about your car, house, or designer diaper bag. Their needs are surprisingly simple: food, warmth, love, and the occasional diaper change. Everything else? That's just extras.

I've seen kids grow up in mansions and in mobile homes that you'd consider unlivable. Want to know a secret? The kids with less often turned out to be more resourceful, more appreciative, and frankly, more interesting. They were collecting eggs from the family chickens while their counterparts were going to Space Camp for the third time.

The One Resource You Can't Renew

Now, let me get personal for a moment. My sister had her first child at 18. Yes, it was tough. Yes, there were struggles. But today? She's spent over two decades watching her kids grow up. She's shared their experiences, related to their challenges, and built a bond that's unbreakable.

Me? I put my career first. My wife and I waited, saved, and focused on our careers. And when we finally decided it was time? We faced fertility issues that led us down the expensive and emotionally draining path of IVF.

Today, I have an awesome son. But there's a 45-year gap between us. My parents might not see him graduate high school. And if I'm being brutally honest, I might not either.

The kicker? All that waiting didn't make me fabulously wealthy and free to spend every moment together. I still do a daily grind but with less energy and less time to enjoy my child.

Timing is Everything

Let's talk biology for a second. Our bodies have a schedule, and it doesn't always align with our financial plans. Having children earlier can reduce the risks associated with later pregnancies and increase your chances of conception without medical intervention.

And let's not forget energy levels. Chasing a toddler in your 20s or 30s is an entirely different ballgame than doing it in your 40s or 50s. Trust me.

It Takes a Village (and a Government)

Now, I know what you're thinking: "But I really can't afford a child right now!" Here's the thing: you're not alone. There are support systems in place that many people overlook:

1. **Government Programs**: Numerous programs, from WIC to Medicaid, are designed to help families with necessities like food and healthcare.
2. **Employer Benefits**: Many companies offer parental leave and flexible working arrangements. Use them!
3. **Family and Community**: Don't underestimate the value of a support network. Grandparents, friends, and neighbors can be lifesavers. And the hand-me-downs may prevent you from buying things for years.

Remember, these resources are valuable regardless of when you have kids or how much money you have. The difference is that by having kids earlier, you're using these supports while also maximizing your time together.

Kids as Your Personal Finance Gurus

Here's an unexpected benefit of early parenthood: it can make you better with money. Nothing motivates you to budget, save, and plan like having another life depending on you. It's like enrolling in a hands-on, high-stakes personal finance course – with a really cute professor.

Parenthood as Professional Motivation

Contrary to popular belief, having kids doesn't have to derail your career. For many, it becomes rocket fuel. When you have mouths to feed, you're often more motivated to advance, seek opportunities, and push yourself professionally. It's amazing how quickly you can climb the ladder when you're not just doing it for yourself.

Young Parents, Young Grandparents

Think about this: by having kids earlier, you're not just impacting your life – you're changing the dynamics for generations. Young grandparents can be more involved, active, and present in their grandchildren's lives. It's a gift that keeps on giving, creating bonds that span decades.

Time is the Ultimate Currency

Look, I'm not saying you should recklessly jump into parenthood without any thought or planning. But I am saying that waiting for the "perfect" financial moment might cost you something far more valuable than money: time.

You can always make more money. You can change careers, get promotions, or win the lottery (I said you could play it, not count on it). But you can't create more time. You can't turn back the clock and have those years of shared experiences and growth.

Having kids, regardless of your financial situation, is a leap of faith. But it's a leap that millions before you have taken, often with far fewer resources than we have today. And you know what? Most of them would say it's the best decision they ever made.

So, if you're on the fence, waiting for that mythical moment when you feel 100% ready – financially, emotionally, whatever – consider this your wake-up call. The time you spend with your kids is the most valuable asset you'll ever have. Start investing in it sooner rather than later. I wish I had.

27

Don't Put Money In Your Kid's Name

When Good Intentions Meet Teenage Logic

Does this sound like a good idea? Your child suddenly turns 18 and instantly has access to thousands of dollars. What could possibly go wrong with that?

If your answer is "everything," congratulations! You've just stumbled upon one of the biggest pitfalls of putting money in your kid's name. Sure, you had visions of responsible saving and wise investments. But your teenager? They're seeing a shiny new car, a lavish spring break trip, or worse.

Remember, we're talking about individuals who might consider a steady diet of ramen noodles a balanced meal plan. Are these really the financial wizards you want in charge of years of your hard-earned savings?

When Free Money Breeds Entitlement

Let me tell you a cautionary tale about a friend of mine. In a burst of generosity (or temporary insanity), he decided to give his son a $500 weekly allowance. Fast forward to college graduation, and Junior faces the harsh reality of a $1,000-per-week job. His response? Outrage at this "unfair" pay rate.

This is what happens when you disconnect money from effort. By putting substantial funds in your child's name, you risk creating a mini-mogul with maxed-out entitlement and zero financial street smarts.

Debunking the Tax Bracket Myth

Now, I know what some of you are thinking. "But what about the tax advantages? Surely, putting money in my kid's name will save me a bundle on taxes!"

Hold on because I'm about to drop a truth bomb: The math doesn't work out the way you think it does.

Yes, your child might be in a lower tax bracket. And yes, there are complex strategies involving family businesses and kiddie Roth IRAs that promise millions in 65 years. But here's the kicker: A dollar in your account will grow exactly the same as a dollar in your child's account over time.

The only difference? You get to keep control of that dollar. And trust me, that control is priceless.

Why Future Millions Don't Justify Present Risks

Let's address those eye-popping projections of how much a small investment will be worth in 65 years. You know the ones - "Invest $1,000 when your child is born, and they'll be millionaires by retirement!"

Sounds great! But here's what they're not telling you. You could achieve the exact same result by keeping that money in your own account and passing it on later. The laws of compound interest don't discriminate based on whose name is on the account. When you die, your kid can inherit your assets and let them grow. That $1,000 can still have 65 years in the market. It just might change hands at some point.

And here's the kicker: There's actually a sneaky tax advantage to keeping those investments in your name. It's called the step-up in basis provision. Sounds fancy, right? Well, it's actually a golden ticket for your heirs.

Here's how it works: Let's say you buy some stocks for $10,000, and by the time you pass away, they're worth $100,000. If you had given those stocks to your child during your lifetime, they'd be on the hook for taxes on that

$90,000 gain when they eventually sell. But if they inherit those same stocks after you're gone? Poof! The IRS magically pretends those stocks were always worth $100,000. Your kid can turn around and sell them the next day without paying a dime in capital gains taxes. It's like the taxman developed amnesia about all those years of growth.

The difference is that you maintain control by keeping it in your name. You can adjust your strategy as circumstances change. You can respond to life's curveballs. And most importantly, you can ensure the money is used wisely when the time comes.

Preserving Your Financial Freedom

Here's something the "put it in your kid's name" crowd often overlooks: financial flexibility. By keeping money in your own accounts, you're not just preserving control - you're preserving options.

Need to pay for an unexpected medical expense? Want to seize a once-in-a-lifetime investment opportunity? With the money in your name, you can make those decisions. With the money in your child's name? You might find yourself in the awkward position of asking your teenager for a loan.

When Custodianship Ends, and Reality Begins

Imagine this scenario. For years, you've been the responsible custodian of your child's account. You've monitored it, managed it, and maybe even bragged about it on social media. Then, suddenly, your child turns 18 (or 21, depending on your state), and poof! Your access disappears.

Now, not only can you not check the balance or influence decisions, but you might also be setting your child up for a financial shock. Suddenly, they're solely responsible for a sum of money they may not be equipped to handle. It's like handing them the keys to a Ferrari when they've just learned to ride a bike.

Why Less Money Can Mean More Growth

Here's a counterintuitive idea. By not putting a large sum of money in your child's name, you might actually be doing them a favor. You're allowing them to experience a more typical financial journey - one where they learn the value of money through earning, saving, and even making mistakes with smaller sums.

This "normal" financial life can teach invaluable lessons that no trust fund can buy. It can foster resilience, creativity, and a genuine understanding of financial responsibility.

Keep Your Money Close and Your Options Open

Look, I get it. The idea of setting your child up for financial success is tempting. It feels good. It might even make you feel like you're winning the parenting game. But the truth is, you can achieve all the same financial goals without putting money in your child's name - and avoid a host of potential pitfalls in the process.

By keeping money in your own accounts, you:

1. Maintain control and flexibility
2. Avoid potential misuse of funds
3. Preserve the same growth potential
4. Allow your child to develop financial responsibility naturally
5. Keep your options open for the future

Remember, good parenting isn't about handing your children a fortune - it's about teaching them how to build their own. And sometimes, the best way to do that is by keeping the purse strings firmly in your own hands. The best financial gift you can give your children isn't a lump sum of cash - it's the knowledge, skills, and values they need to create their own financial success story.

VIII

Investing

The old rules of investing might be holding you back from real wealth. Let's explore alternative investment strategies that go beyond the standard advice. It's time to think outside the index fund box.

28

Be An Early Adopter

When Playing It Safe Keeps You Poor

Here's the opposite of following tried and true advice. I think you should absolutely be an early adopter when it comes to investing. It sounds like reckless gambling advice, but I've thought about this a lot lately. The investing landscape has changed dramatically, and those who stick to the old rules might find themselves left in the dust.

Why Today's Winners Move Faster

Remember when becoming an industry titan took decades? Those days are gone. In your grandparents' era, building an empire meant laying railroad tracks or constructing factories. Today? A kid in a dorm room can create a billion-dollar company before they've even graduated.

    The tech sector moves at warp speed. Companies scale faster than the news gets reported. So, by the time your favorite financial guru is recommending a stock, the real money has already been made.

How the Big Boys Are Hoarding the Good Stuff

Here's a dirty little secret of modern investing: by the time you and I can buy shares in the "next big thing," it's probably not so "next" anymore. Private equity and venture capital firms are snatching up the most promising companies long before they hit the public markets.

Remember Uber's IPO? By the time the average investor could get in on the action, the company was already valued at billions. The early speculators had already hit the jackpot, leaving us retail investors to fight over the scraps.

Small Bets, Big Potential

Now, I'm not suggesting you bet your life savings on the latest crypto-AI-blockchain-AR-VR-graphene-neurolink startup. That's a one-way ticket to financial ruin. Instead, think of early adoption as your "satellite strategy" – small, speculative bets that orbit your core investment portfolio.

The beauty of this approach? While your main investments chug along at a respectable 8-10% annual return, your satellite investments have the potential for explosive growth. We're talking 1,000% or even 10,000% returns. It's like having a lottery ticket based on insight rather than pure luck.

Why Nobody Knows the Future (And Why That's Okay)

Here's the thing about being an early adopter: if it were easy to predict the next big thing, everyone would do it. The fact that it's challenging is precisely what creates the opportunity.

Maybe quantum computing will be the next world-changing technology. It's more likely it'll be something we haven't even imagined yet. The point isn't to have a crystal ball; it's to be in the game when the next revolution happens.

Using Tech to Inform Your Investments

Want to get an edge? Start using emerging technologies in your personal or business life. By becoming an early adopter in practice, you'll gain insights that can inform your investment decisions.

Maybe you'll discover that a new AI tool is revolutionizing your workflow or that a new material is solving problems you didn't even know you had. These firsthand experiences can give you the confidence to invest before the crowd catches on.

Why Waiting for Proof Can Cost You

Ever heard of FOMO – Fear of Missing Out? In investing, there's a dangerous flip side: the fear of getting in too early. But here's the truth: if you wait for ironclad proof that a technology is world-changing, you've probably already missed the biggest gains.

Look at artificial intelligence. Those who invested in AI companies a year ago have seen their investments skyrocket. Those who waited for "more data"? They're buying in at the top, hoping they haven't missed the entire party.

Why You Need Some Wild Cards in Your Portfolio

Let's talk about moonshots – those high-risk, high-reward investments that could change everything. Remember, you don't need every speculative investment to pay off. Just one "1,000x" winner can make up for a lot of losers.

Think of it this way: if you invest $1,000 in ten speculative plays, and nine of them go to zero, but one turns into $100,000, you're still up 900%. Try getting that return from an index fund.

Lessons from a Revolutionary Prediction

Let me share a personal anecdote. When the first iPhone was unveiled, I wrote an article predicting it would become the standard for phone technology. I even made the bold claim that Apple might even sell a staggering 20 million devices.

In hindsight, that prediction was laughably conservative. For those wondering, Apple has sold over 2.3 billion iPhones so far. But it illustrates an important point: even when you spot a revolutionary technology, it's hard to grasp its full potential. The lesson? When you see something truly groundbreaking, it might be even bigger than you imagine.

How to Be an Early Adopter (Without Losing Your Shirt)

So, how do you put this into practice? Here's your action plan:

1. Allocate a small percentage of your portfolio (say, 5-10%) to speculative investments.
2. Dive into emerging technologies. Use them, understand them, live them.
3. Stay informed about startups and new tech trends.
4. Be prepared to lose your entire investment in these speculative plays.
5. Remember: you're not aiming for a 100% success rate. You're swinging for the fences, knowing you'll miss more often than you hit.

Fortune Favors the Bold (and the Early)

Look, I get it. Being an early adopter feels risky. It goes against the grain of traditional financial advice. But in a world where technology is reshaping entire industries overnight, playing it safe might be the riskiest move of all.

You don't need to abandon your core investment strategy. Keep maxing out that 401(k), maintain a diversified portfolio, and all that good stuff. But carve out a small portion of your investments for moonshots. Be the early adopter. Be the one who saw it coming. When the next big thing hits, you don't want to sit on the sidelines, wondering what could have been. You want to be in the game, reaping the rewards of your foresight and courage.

29

Buy Cryptocurrencies

Cryptocurrency's Rise to Legitimacy

If you thought the stock market was a roller coaster, crypto is like strapping yourself to a rocket and hoping you land on the moon instead of crashing back to Earth. But here's the revelation: you should be buying it.

How Crypto Crashed the Finance Party

Remember when Bitcoin was just for tech nerds and people buying sketchy stuff online? Well, those days are long gone. Cryptocurrencies have gone from the financial world's ugly duckling to the belle of the ball. And while there are still plenty of crypto coins out there worth less than the electricity it takes to Google them, the big players like Bitcoin have proven they've got more lives than a cat in a bubble wrap factory.

Your Ticket to the Big Leagues

Here's where it gets really juicy. While traditional finance keeps playing bouncer at the exclusive investment club, crypto is throwing a block party, and everyone's invited. Got an internet connection and a few bucks to spare?

Congratulations, you're now playing in the same league as the big shots.

Why Traditional Finance is Moving Slower Than Your Grandma on Facebook

Let's face it: the old guard of finance moves at the speed of a frightened baby slowed down by regulators. By the time your financial advisor finishes his PowerPoint presentation on why crypto might be worth considering, early adopters have already bought a Lambo with their Bitcoin gains. Their cautious approach might keep you "safe," but it also might keep you from retiring before you're old enough to forget why you wanted to retire in the first place.

Because Your Portfolio Needs More Than Just Stocks and Bonds

If your idea of a diverse portfolio is splitting your money between Apple and Microsoft, I have news for you. Traditional investments are starting to move in lockstep. Crypto, on the other hand, dances to its own beat. Sometimes, it moves with the market. Other times, it moves against it. But its unpredictable independence is what makes it compelling.

How to Play Crypto Without Losing Your Shirt (Or Your Mind)

Now, let's be clear: investing in crypto is about as safe as juggling chainsaws. But here's the secret sauce - if you only juggle with chainsaws you can afford to drop, suddenly it's not so scary. This has to fit within your "satellite" strategy. Invest only what you can lose, and you've turned a potential financial catastrophe into a thrilling game of chance.

Confessions of a Recovering Crypto Skeptic

Let me tell you a little story about yours truly. It pains me to think about the many times I passed on Bitcoin. At $20, $100, $200 - each time, I pushed it away like a plate of broccoli. It wasn't until Bitcoin hit $1,700 that I started paying attention, but even then, I listened to the "experts" calling it a fad and promising it was headed back to zero.

I finally took the plunge at $12,000, fully prepared to write it off as a very expensive lesson in FOMO. Fast forward to today, with Bitcoin cruising around $70,000, my only regret is not actually buying more. The moral of the story? Even we late bloomers can still catch the crypto train - just make sure you're not using your retirement fund as the ticket.

Crypto's Mainstream Moment

We're witnessing a seismic shift in how the world views crypto. Major companies are adding Bitcoin to their balance sheets faster than you can say "bull run." Payment processors are jumping on the crypto bandwagon, and traditional banks are exploring digital currencies like teenagers discovering social media. The crypto revolution isn't coming - it's here.

Because Bitcoin Isn't the Only Animal in This Digital Jungle

While Bitcoin's been hogging the spotlight, there's a whole cast of supporting characters waiting in the wings. New cryptocurrencies are popping up all the time, and trying to pick the next big winner is about as easy as finding a specific grain of sand on a beach.

But here's the kicker: while Bitcoin's busy being the superstar of cryptocurrencies, some of these supporting actors are quietly turning into the next big thing. They might not have the star power yet, but they've got potential that could make Bitcoin look like a has-been child actor.

Now, I know what you're thinking: "How am I supposed to know which crypto is the next big thing and which one is just digital snake oil?" You can't, but here's something that can help.

Mixing Your Digital Drinks for Maximum Flavor

Welcome to the world of crypto index services, helping you sample a little bit of everything. Here's how it works: instead of trying to pick the winning horse, you spread your bets across the whole field. These services take your investment and sprinkle it across a smorgasbord of cryptocurrencies. You don't have to know your Ethereum from your elbow to get started.

Slow and Steady Wins the Race (Sometimes)

Now, here's where it gets really interesting. Instead of throwing your life savings into this crypto cocktail all at once (please don't do that, I beg you), you can play it cool with a little strategy called dollar-cost averaging.

It works like this: you set aside a small amount of "play money" each month - and I'm talking fun money here, not your rent or your kid's college fund - and invest it regularly into one of these crypto index services. It's like feeding a slot machine, but instead of pulling the lever, you're potentially building a diverse crypto portfolio.

Some months, your money might buy you a treasure trove of tokens. In other months, it might feel like you're buying digital air. But over time, you're spreading out your risk and potentially catching the next big thing before it hits.

What Big Finance Says vs. What It Does (Or How to Spot a Financial Hypocrite)

Here's where it gets really interesting. Big financial institutions are standing on their soapboxes, wagging their fingers about the risks of crypto. Meanwhile, behind the scenes, they're stuffing their pockets with cryptocurrencies faster than a squirrel hoarding nuts.

Let's look at the receipts:

- BlackRock, the world's largest asset manager, launched a Bitcoin ETF

that gobbled up over $23.7 billion in assets. Oh, and they're sitting on $10 billion worth of Bitcoin for their clients calling it a "unique diversifier."
- Fidelity's Bitcoin ETF? It has $11.2 billion in assets. Their own Bitcoin stash? A cool $5 billion.
- JPMorgan Chase's CEO once called Bitcoin a fraud. Now, they're offering crypto funds to wealthy clients with over $1 billion in crypto exposure.
- Goldman Sachs launched a Digital Assets Platform handling $3 billion in crypto transactions monthly. That's more than just embracing crypto.

The takeaway? While these financial bigwigs are publicly preaching caution, they're privately betting on crypto. What I'm hearing is, "Do as I say, not as I do."

Join the Digital Gold Rush (Or Risk Being Left in the Financial Stone Age)

The crypto revolution isn't just knocking on the door; it's kicked it down and is redecorating the living room. Sure, there are risks - but in finance, the biggest risk is often missing out on the next big thing.

The actions of the financial giants speak louder than their cautionary words. These folks have built empires by sniffing out opportunities early, and right now, their noses are leading them straight to crypto.

So, here's the million-coin question: are you going to listen to what the big financial institutions say, or are you going to watch what they do? Because while they're telling you to be careful, they're stockpiling crypto. Please do your research, know your risk tolerance, and consider whether it's time for you to join the digital gold rush.

30

Don't Worry About Risk Tolerance

How Feelings Sabotage Your Finances

Let's talk about a dirty little secret in the world of investing. Do you know those risk tolerance questionnaires that investment professionals love to hand out? They're irrelevant.

You've probably seen the ones I'm talking about. "How would you feel if your portfolio dropped 20% in a month?" As if your feelings have any bearing on what the market's going to do or what you should do about it.

Here's the truth: your personal risk tolerance should not determine your investment strategy. What really matters? Time. Cold, hard, unfeeling time.

When "Aggressive" Is Just Right

When I joined my father's financial planning practice, I noticed something peculiar. Every twenty-something client got the same advice: go aggressive. It didn't matter if they were a sky-diving adrenaline junkie or wore bubble-wrap parkas.

Why? Because when you're decades away from retirement, your portfolio should be aggressive. Your personal feelings about risk are irrelevant when you've got 40 years for the market to do its thing.

It's Not About Age, It's About Time

Now, here's where it gets interesting. Even if you're in your 40s or 50s, a significant chunk of your portfolio should still be playing offense, not defense. Why? Retirement isn't a single point in time - it's a twenty, thirty, or more-year journey.

If you're 55 with a portfolio that'll need to support you until you're 85, guess what? A large portion of that money has a 30-year time horizon. It should be out there working hard, not hiding in low-yield bonds because you get queasy at the thought of market volatility.

Why Your Feelings Don't Factor

Let's be real for a moment. If you're investing for a goal that's decades away, your day-to-day emotions about the market are about as relevant as your opinion on silent films.

Those questionnaires that ask, "What would you do if your portfolio dropped 20%?" Here's the correct answer: Nothing. You'd do absolutely nothing because if your time horizon is measured in decades, short-term market movements are just noise.

When Short-Term Goals Change the Game

Now, let's switch gears. Say you're saving for a house down payment you'll need in 12 to 18 months. Suddenly, your risk tolerance matters, right? Wrong again.

In this scenario, your investment strategy should be as boring as watching paint dry. We're talking cash, money market funds, or maybe a short-term government bond if you're feeling antsy. Why? Because your time horizon is short, and capital preservation is key.

Your personal ability to stomach market swings is irrelevant. What matters is that you need that money soon, and you need it to be there when you need it.

The Only Investment Clock That Matters

Here's the real rule of investment selection: It's not about your risk tolerance. It's about your time horizon.

- 20+ years until you need the money? Aggressive all the way.
- 10-20 years? It's still pretty aggressive, with maybe a dash of moderation.
- 5-10 years? Now, we're talking about a more balanced approach.
- Less than 5 years? Time to start playing it safe.

Your personal feelings about risk don't enter into this equation at all. It's all about when you need the money and what the historical data tells us about market performance over various time frames.

Putting Time Over Temperament

So, how do we put this into practice? Here's your action plan:

1. Ignore those risk tolerance questionnaires.
2. For each of your financial goals, identify the time horizon. When will you need this money?
3. Based on that time horizon, not your personal feelings, allocate your investments. The longer the horizon, the more aggressive you can (and should) be.
4. Resist the urge to react to short-term market movements for long-term goals.
5. For short-term goals (less than 5 years), prioritize capital preservation over growth, regardless of how you feel about risk.

Time Trumps Temperament

Look, I get it. It's hard to ignore your emotions when it comes to money. But successful investing isn't about feeling good in the moment. It's about achieving your long-term financial goals.

By focusing on your time horizon rather than your risk tolerance, you're letting cold, hard data drive your decisions, not fleeting emotions. It might not always feel comfortable, but it's the surest path to financial success.

Remember, in the world of investing, time isn't just money - it's everything. So stop worrying about your risk tolerance and start paying attention to your investment clock. Your future wealthy self will thank you.

31

Don't Use An Index Fund

Unmasking the Index Fund's Performance Claims

Let's start with a statement that will leave all my fellow financial independence friends fuming: index funds probably can't deliver what you need. Yes, I am about to challenge one of our most sacred cows.

You've probably heard the oft-repeated claim that index funds outperform 80% of actively managed funds. It's a statistic so ingrained in the investing zeitgeist that it's treated as gospel. But here's the kicker: this comparison is about as fair as a heavyweight boxer taking on the neighborhood kid.

Why the Deck is Stacked

Let's break this down. Most index funds, like those tracking the S&P 500, are 100% invested in equities. They rise and fall with the market, no holds barred. But here's the catch: many of the mutual funds they're compared against aren't playing the same game.

Many actively managed funds hold cash positions or bonds to manage risk and match specific investor profiles. It's like comparing a sprinter to a marathon runner - sure, they're both runners, but they're optimized for entirely different races.

When you remove these differently structured funds from the comparison, suddenly, our index fund hero isn't looking so heroic. In fact, it's often sitting squarely in the middle of the pack.

When the Tide Goes Out

Now, don't get me wrong. When the market's on a bull run, being fully invested in equities via an index fund feels great. You're riding the wave, seeing your portfolio swell with each market uptick. But what happens when the tide turns?

We've seen the market take 50% nosedives before. If you're young and have decades ahead of you, this might be a bump in the road. But if you're nearing retirement or already drawing on your assets, it's less of a bump and more of a sinkhole. Suddenly, that fund with cash or bond positions seems mighty attractive.

Reinventing the Wheel

Here's where it gets really interesting. Many index fund devotees recognize this risk and attempt to mitigate it by adding bonds or cash equivalents to their portfolios. But in doing so, they're essentially creating a makeshift version of the very mutual funds they were trying to outperform in the first place.

It's like refusing to buy a car because you think you can build a better one, only to end up with something that looks suspiciously like what's already on the market - just with more of your own blood, sweat, and tears invested.

Not All Indexes Are Created Equal

Let's talk about the elephant in the room: market-cap weighting. Most popular index funds, like those tracking the S&P 500, are weighted by market capitalization. This means the biggest companies make up the largest portion of the fund.

But here's the rub: these behemoths might have less room for growth precisely because they're already so large. It's like betting on the frontrunner in a race - sure, they're in the lead now, but how much faster can they really go?

There are alternatives, like equal-weighted funds, that might offer more growth potential by giving smaller companies an equal share of the pie. Or you might want factor-based weightings where some companies are adjusted based on specific objectives like growth, value, volatility management, or even momentum. It's worth considering if you're looking for that extra edge.

When More Really Is More

Now, let me introduce you to another investing option: equity plus funds. These funds aim to give you the performance of the index and then some by investing the remainder in bonds.

Imagine getting all the upside of the market plus an extra 3-5% on top. During bull markets, you're outpacing the index. And when things go south? That bond cushion helps soften the blow.

One Size Doesn't Fit All

The fundamental issue with the index fund craze is that it assumes one size fits all when investing. But your financial goals, risk tolerance, and life stage are uniquely yours. A 22-year-old fresh out of college has very different needs than a 60-year-old on the brink of retirement.

Blindly following the "index funds are best" mantra ignores these crucial differences. It's like prescribing the same medication to every patient, regardless of their symptoms.

Embracing Complexity

If you're holding anything in your portfolio besides an index fund - be it a bond fund, a single stock, or even cash - you're already not fully subscribing to the index-only philosophy. And that's okay! In fact, it might be better than okay.

By thoughtfully constructing a portfolio that aligns with your specific goals, you're taking control of your financial future. You're acknowledging that while the market as a whole tends to go up over time, your individual needs might require a more nuanced approach.

Think Beyond the Index

Look, I'm not saying index funds are evil or that you should liquidate all your total market funds tomorrow. What I am saying is this: don't let the simplicity of index investing lull you into complacency. Don't assume a fund that includes everything provides you with everything you need.

Take the time to understand your options. Consider your personal goals and your investment timeline. Look into equal-weighted funds, equity plus funds, carefully selected actively managed funds, or non-equity funds that align with your objectives.

Remember, the goal isn't to beat some arbitrary benchmark or to have the lowest expense ratio. The goal is to build a portfolio that works for you and helps you sleep at night while still reaching your financial goals.

32

Ignore Investment Expenses

How Penny-Pinching Can Leave You Penniless

Now, I know what some people want to say, "But Peter, the point of index funds is their low costs." So, here's a statement that will get every armchair investor angry: I don't care about fund expenses. That's right. In fact, I think the widespread obsession with low-fee funds is one of the biggest mistakes investors make today. This fixation on fund expenses isn't just misguided - it could be robbing your financial future.

When Comparison Shopping Goes Wrong

Here's the thing about fund expenses: they matter when you're comparing identical funds. If Fund A and Fund B are both tracking the S&P 500 in exactly the same way, and A has lower fees, then sure, go with A. It's a no-brainer.

However, the real danger comes when comparing very different types of funds based on their expenses. A fund that researches companies overseas is going to have different expenses than a fund that only invests domestically. A fund that employs doctors to analyze biotech or pharmaceutical products is going to be more expensive than an index fund.

Comparing funds based solely on their expense ratios is like choosing transportation solely on how much fuel it burns. Even if a flight is cheap and fast, you might rationalize riding your bicycle.

Why Net Returns Trump Everything

Let's cut to the chase: the only number that really matters is how much money ends up in your pocket. It's the investment equivalent of "Show me the money!"

Imagine I offer you two investments:

1. **Fund A**: 5% annual return, 0.1% expense ratio
2. **Fund B**: 7% annual return, 0.5% expense ratio

Which one would you choose? If you're still stuck on expenses, you might be tempted to go with Fund A. But here's a wake-up call: Fund B will make you richer, period. The extra 2% in returns more than compensates for the higher fees.

When High Fees Lead to High Returns

Let me tell you a quick story about my father. In retirement, he invested in a fund focused on nursing home real estate. This fund had an eye-watering expense ratio of 5% - enough to give most fee-obsessed investors a heart attack.

But here's the kicker: it consistently netted 10% annually. Even after those hefty fees, investors were pocketing a tidy 10% annual return. In a low-interest-rate environment, that's nothing to sneeze at.

The moral of the story? If a fund is delivering the returns you need and fits your risk profile, who cares about the expenses?

Why The Store's Costs Don't Matter To You

Think about it this way: when you're buying groceries, do you care how much the store paid for the products? Of course not! You care about the price you're paying and the quality you're getting.

Investing is no different. Whether a fund manager is able to keep their costs low is irrelevant to you as an investor. What matters is the price you're paying (the expense ratio) relative to what you're getting (the returns).

If Store A sells minestrone soup for $2 a can and Store B sells it for $1.50, you're going to buy from Store B - even if Store A got a better wholesale price. The same logic applies to your investments.

What You're Missing While Counting Pennies

Here's where the expense ratio obsession really bites you: opportunity cost. While you're painstakingly comparing expense ratios down to the hundredth of a percent, you might be missing out on funds with superior strategies, better management, or exposure to high-growth sectors.

In other words, you're so focused on not losing money to fees that you're blind to opportunities to make money through returns. It's like being so worried about the cost of admission to a gold mine that you never go in and start digging.

Why Cheap Isn't Always Cheerful

Another problem with the low-fee fixation is that it often leads to over-concentration in a handful of popular, low-cost index funds. While these can be great core holdings, true diversification often requires venturing into more specialized and, sometimes, more expensive funds.

A portfolio of nothing but rock-bottom fee index funds might look great on paper, but it might also leave you dangerously exposed to market downturns or missing out on growth opportunities in specific sectors or regions.

Focus on What Really Matters

Look, I'm not saying you should completely ignore expenses. They're a factor to consider, especially when all else is equal. But they should be way, way down on your list of priorities when evaluating investments.

Instead, focus on:

1. **Net returns**: What's actually ending up in your pocket?
2. **Risk profile**: Does this investment align with your risk tolerance and goals?
3. **Strategy**: Does the fund's approach make sense given market conditions and your investment thesis?
4. **Diversification**: How does this fund fit into your overall portfolio?

Remember, the goal of investing isn't to pay the least in fees. It's to make the most money possible within your risk tolerance. Sometimes, that means paying a bit more in expenses for a lot more in returns. After all, no one ever got rich by saving money on fund fees. But plenty of people have missed out on fortunes by being penny-wise and pound-foolish.

33

Don't Invest Only In What You Know

Debunking the "Know What You Own" Myth

For years, we've been fed the line that you should "invest in what you know." It sounds smart, doesn't it? Do you drive a Ford? Then maybe you should have some Ford stock. Do you have a good grasp on real estate? Then maybe you should invest in some. Don't understand stock options? Then stay far away. But you know what? Sometimes, the best investments are the ones you don't understand.

Especially in today's complex financial world, this advice might be steering you away from some of the most powerful wealth-building tools available.

Leveraging Other People's Knowledge

Here's some truth. You don't need to understand how a car engine works to benefit from driving. So why should investing be any different?

When you invest in complex financial products, you're not going it alone. You're leveraging the expertise of financial professionals who eat, sleep, and breathe these investments.

Uncovering Hidden Gems

Let's talk about some of these mysterious beasts: Guaranteed lifetime withdrawal benefits, market-neutral funds, long-short strategies, Smart Beta, and derivatives. Sound like financial gibberish? That's okay. What matters is the benefits they can provide.

These complex products often offer unique advantages that simpler investments can't match. Guaranteed minimum returns in a volatile market? Yes, please. Steady returns regardless of market direction? Sign me up.

Just because you don't understand the inner workings doesn't mean these products aren't perfect for you. It's like not understanding how Netflix's algorithm works but still enjoying a perfectly tailored movie night.

When Understanding Holds You Back

Here's a mind-bender for you: your limited knowledge might actually be limiting your investment options. If you only invest in what you understand, and you only understand a handful of companies or industries, you're leaving a world of opportunities on the table.

When Knowledge Isn't Power

Let's flip the script for a moment. Just because you understand something doesn't mean it's a good investment. Remember Blockbuster? Blackberry? Kodak? Plenty of people understood these businesses perfectly - right up until they became obsolete.

Understanding a company or industry doesn't give you a crystal ball. Sometimes, it can even blind you to changing trends or disruptive technologies.

Your Guide In Uncharted Territory

Now, I'm not suggesting you blindly throw your money at every complex financial product out there. That's where professional advice comes in.

A good financial advisor or broker can be your translator in the world of complex investments. They can help you understand the potential benefits and risks, even if you don't grasp every technical detail.

It's like having a knowledgeable guide on an expedition through unfamiliar terrain. You don't need to know how to read a topographical map or use a compass—you just need to trust your guide and enjoy the journey.

Growing Your Financial IQ

Here's another secret. Investing in things you don't initially understand can actually make you smarter over time. As you dip your toes into unfamiliar waters, you'll naturally start to learn more about these investments.

It's like learning a new language through immersion. At first, it's all gibberish. But gradually, you start to pick up words, then phrases, and before you know it, you're conversing like a local.

Eyes Wide Open

Let's address the reality that investing in things you don't fully understand comes with risks. But here's the thing: all investing involves risk. Even sticking your money under your mattress risks losing value to inflation.

The key is to understand those risks in relation to your investment goals. You don't need to understand the intricacies of options trading to know whether you're comfortable with the potential risks and rewards.

Embracing the Unknown

Look, I get it. Investing in the unfamiliar can feel scary. We're hardwired to fear the unknown. But in the world of investing, that fear might be holding you back from incredible opportunities.

Here's your new mantra: "I don't need to understand everything to benefit from it." Remember, the most successful investors aren't necessarily the ones who understand every detail. They're the ones who know how to leverage expertise, balance risk with reward, and stay open to new opportunities - even if those opportunities come wrapped in a layer of complexity.

34

Don't Be A Contrarian Investor

The Allure of Going Against the Grain

We all love a good underdog story. There's something irresistibly appealing about the idea of zigging when everyone else zags, of being the lone wolf who sees what the herd is missing. In the world of investing, this mindset has a name: contrarian investing.

The contrarian investor looks at a soaring stock and thinks, "It's too high. It must come down." They see a plummeting market and think, "Time to buy!" It sounds smart, doesn't it? After all, we've all heard Warren Buffett's famous advice to be "fearful when others are greedy and greedy when others are fearful."

But here's a thought that might just rock your financial world: What if being a contrarian is actually holding you back?

The High Cost of Being Right (Eventually)

Let me tell you a personal story that might sound familiar. Back in 2004, I was eyeing the housing market. Everyone was saying it was too hot and that prices couldn't possibly go higher. Being the clever contrarian I thought I was, I decided to wait it out. I rented a less-than-luxurious apartment, smugly waiting for the market to crash so I could swoop in and buy at the bottom.

Fast forward several years, and I finally caved. I bought at what turned out to be the peak of the market. Ouch.

Here's the kicker: If I had ignored the contrarian voice in my head and bought a couple of years earlier when everyone was piling in, I would have enjoyed two years of appreciation before the downturn. Yes, I still would have lost value when the market crashed, but I would've still been better off.

The lesson? Sometimes, the crowd isn't wrong – at least not for long enough to make your contrarian stance worthwhile.

Riding the Wave

Have you ever heard of momentum investing? It's the opposite of contrarian investing, and it's based on a simple principle: What goes up often continues to go up, at least for a while.

It might not sound as intellectually satisfying as identifying undervalued assets, but here's a hard truth: Momentum often works. Stocks that are rising tend to keep rising. Markets that are bullish often stay bullish longer than you'd expect.

By always trying to be the smartest person in the room, always looking for the turn, you might be missing out on significant gains. Would you rather be right and poor or wrong and rich?

The Psychological Toll of Swimming Upstream

Being a contrarian isn't just potentially bad for your wallet – it's exhausting for your mind. Constantly going against the crowd, always doubting the prevailing wisdom, can be mentally draining.

This psychological strain can lead to poor decision-making. When you're always on edge, always waiting for the other shoe to drop, you're more likely to make impulsive moves based on fear rather than sound strategy. You can easily find yourself embracing the philosophy, "If you can't beat 'em, join 'em."

The Timing Trap

One of the biggest challenges for contrarian investors is timing. It's not enough to identify an overvalued or undervalued asset – you must time your move perfectly to profit.

Guess what? Timing the market consistently is about as easy as predicting the weather a year in advance. Even professional fund managers rarely do it reliably. For us mere mortals, it's a game we're almost certain to lose in the long run.

The Opportunity Cost of Contrarianism

While you're sitting on the sidelines, waiting for the perfect contrarian play, the market is moving. Those "overvalued" stocks might just keep climbing. That "frothy" market might froth for years before it pops.

Every moment you spend waiting for your contrarian view to play out is a moment you could have been in the market, benefiting from its overall upward trajectory. Remember, in the long run, markets tend to rise. By trying to outsmart short-term movements, you might be outsmarting yourself out of long-term gains.

Informed Trend-Following

Now, I'm not suggesting you should blindly follow every market trend. That's a recipe for buying high and selling low – exactly what we're trying to avoid. Instead, consider a middle ground: informed trend-following.

This approach involves:

1. Recognizing prevailing market trends
2. Understanding the fundamental reasons behind these trends
3. Participating in the trend while it's strong

4. Having an exit strategy for when the trend shows real signs of reversing

This way, you're not ignoring your analytical skills or blindly following the crowd. You're using your knowledge to ride waves intelligently rather than always trying to predict the next big wave.

Don't Let Contrarianism Sink Your Wealth

Being a contrarian can feel good. It can make you feel smarter than the average investor. But at the end of the day, the goal of investing isn't to be right – it's to be richer.

Sometimes, the masses are right. Sometimes, that stock is going up because the company is genuinely performing well. Sometimes, the market is rising because economic fundamentals are strong.

Instead of always trying to be the lone wolf, consider running with the pack – at least some of the time. Keep your eyes open and do your research, but don't be afraid to go with the flow when the evidence supports it. After all, would you rather be the smug guy who predicted the crash or the guy who made money before, during, and after it?

35

Don't Diversify Your Portfolio

The Myth of Safety in Numbers

We've all been fed the line that diversification is the holy grail of investing. "Don't put all your eggs in one basket," they say. You probably instinctively say it whenever you hear "eggs" or "basket." You've heard it so much that you never even question it. Diversification keeps you safe and reduces your risk. So, what's the problem then? Well, diversification might be killing your chances of achieving true wealth. What if that advice is keeping you from the golden goose?

As Warren Buffett, arguably the greatest investor of our time, once said, "Diversification is protection against ignorance. It makes little sense if you know what you are doing."

When Everything Falls Together

Here's a dirty little secret about diversification. In times of crisis, it often fails spectacularly. Remember 2008? Stocks, bonds, real estate - everything took a nosedive together. Your carefully diversified portfolio? It all wet the bed at the same time.

The truth is, in our globalized economy, assets are more correlated than ever. Owning a tech stock in Silicon Valley and a farm in a frontier market might seem diversified, but when the market catches a cold, they both start sneezing.

Concentrated Bets and Big Wins

Now, let's talk about the big boys - the billionaire investors who've made their fortunes through concentrated bets. These folks aren't spreading their money thin; they're going all-in on their best ideas.

Take Mark Cuban, for instance. He's famously said, "Diversification is for idiots. ... You can't diversify enough to know what you're doing." Cuban advocates for investing heavily in one or two things you're passionate about and knowledgeable about.

Why You Need Some High-Risk, High-Reward Plays

Here's a thought that might make you uncomfortable: what if you're diversifying away your chances of life-changing wealth?

Think about the early Apple adopters or the folks who bought Amazon stock in the '90s. These "moonshot" investments turned ordinary people into millionaires. As Peter Thiel, co-founder of PayPal, puts it, "The biggest secret in venture capital is that the best investment in a successful fund equals or outperforms the entire rest of the fund combined."

Adding Some Spice to Your Portfolio

I'm not suggesting you bet the farm on the next hot cryptocurrency. But hopefully, you're starting to see the value of having a satellite strategy with part of your portfolio to take on some high-risk, high-reward investments. Then, you don't have to be afraid to have a few speculative bets that could potentially skyrocket.

When Less is More

There's a growing trend in the investment world called concentrated mutual funds. These are funds that hold only 10-20 stocks instead of hundreds. They're betting on quality over quantity, and many are outperforming their more diversified counterparts.

As Joel Greenblatt, a successful fund manager and author, puts it, "You can't own too many stocks. If you have 100 stocks, you're not going to lose much money, but you're not going to make much either."

Big Names Backing Concentration

It's not just maverick investors advocating for concentration. Even Jack Bogle, the founder of Vanguard and a long-time proponent of index investing, has acknowledged the potential of concentration. He once said, "If you have trouble imagining a 20% loss in the stock market, you shouldn't be in stocks."

The implication? True wealth-building often requires taking on more risk than broad diversification allows.

Rethinking Your Approach to Risk

Yes, I get it. The idea of concentrating your investments is scary. We've been conditioned to see diversification as the ultimate safety net. But what if that net is actually a cage, keeping you from reaching your full financial potential?

I'm not saying you should throw caution to the wind and put all your money in the latest meme stock. But maybe, just maybe, it's time to reconsider how spread out your investments really need to be.

As the legendary investor Philip Fisher once said, "The stock market is filled with individuals who know the price of everything but the value of nothing." Don't let the fear of short-term volatility keep you from potentially life-changing returns.

So, here's your challenge: take a hard look at your portfolio. Are you diversified to the point of mediocrity? Could you benefit from making a few concentrated bets on your highest-conviction ideas?

Remember, in the world of investing, playing it too safe can be the riskiest move of all. Sometimes, you need to concentrate to accumulate.

36

Don't Rebalance Your Portfolio

The Sacred Cow of Portfolio Management

If you've ever dipped your toe into the world of investing, you've probably heard this piece of advice more times than you can count: "Don't forget to rebalance your portfolio!" It's repeated so often that you'd think failing to rebalance would be akin to abandoning your investments altogether. But what if I told you that this financial wisdom might be stunting your wealth growth?

Brace yourself because we're about to tip over one of the sacred cows of investing.

Where the Real Money Grows

Let's start with a fundamental truth that even the most conservative financial advisor can't deny: over the long haul, stocks outperform bonds. It's not even close. We're talking about the difference between a rocket ship and a horse-drawn carriage.

So, here's a wild idea: if stocks perform better, why on earth would you want to keep shifting money out of them and into bonds? It's like benching your star player in the middle of their hot streak.

"But what about risk?" Well, let's talk about that.

The Risk of Playing It Safe

Yes, bonds are generally considered safer than stocks. But "safer" doesn't always mean "better." We've discussed that if you're 30, 40, or even 50 years old, you don't really need to be playing it safe with a significant portion of your portfolio. It's like wearing water wings in the kiddie pool. You're protecting yourself from a risk that, given your time horizon, isn't really a threat.

The Compounding Conundrum

Here's where it gets really interesting. When you let your portfolio ride without rebalancing, you're allowing the magic of compounding to work its full effect on your best-performing assets. It's like letting a snowball roll down a hill - the bigger it gets, the faster it grows.

By constantly rebalancing, you're essentially stopping that snowball halfway down the hill, scraping off some snow, and starting it over. Sure, you've got a more "balanced" set of snowballs, but you've interrupted the incredible growth potential of your winner.

The Data Doesn't Lie

Now, I know what you're thinking. "This sounds great in theory, but what does the data say?" I'm glad you asked.

A study by Vanguard looked at portfolio returns from 1926 to 2009, comparing annually rebalanced portfolios with those that were never rebalanced. The result? The never-rebalanced portfolio actually outperformed, ending up with 2.3% more wealth on average.

Another study by Goldman Sachs examined the performance of a 60/40 stock/bond portfolio from 1926 to 2014. The never-rebalanced portfolio grew to $4,040,000, while the annually rebalanced portfolio only reached

$2,990,000. That's a difference of over a million dollars!

The Hidden Costs of Rebalancing

Let's talk about something that often gets overlooked in the rebalancing debate: costs. Every time you rebalance, you're potentially incurring transaction fees and, even worse, capital gains taxes.

The Market Timing Trap

Here's another dirty little secret about rebalancing: it requires you to time the market. And let me tell you, if there's one thing that's harder than predicting the weather, it's predicting the stock market.

When you rebalance, you're essentially saying, "I think it's time to sell this asset that's been performing well and buy more of this underperforming one." But what if that outperforming asset is just getting started on a bull run? What if the underperforming one is on its way to becoming obsolete?

You're not just moving money around - you're making a bet on the future direction of these assets. And unless you've got a crystal ball tucked away somewhere, that's a dangerous game to play.

The Behavioral Finance Pitfall

Let's get psychological for a moment. A lot of the drive to rebalance comes from our human need for control and our aversion to volatility. We see our portfolio getting "unbalanced," and it makes us uncomfortable. So, we tinker with it to make ourselves feel better.

But here's the thing: the market doesn't care about your comfort. In fact, being comfortable often means you're not taking enough risk to generate significant returns. It's like trying to get in shape without ever breaking a sweat. It might feel nice, but it's not going to get you results.

The Diversification Dilemma

Now, I'm not saying diversification isn't important. It can be helpful. But if you've set up a well-diversified portfolio to begin with, do you really need to keep fiddling with it?

Think of it like planting a garden. You carefully choose a variety of plants that will thrive in your climate and soil. You don't then dig them up every few months and rearrange them. You let them grow.

When Rebalancing Makes Sense

I'm not completely against rebalancing. There are times when it can make sense:

1. When you're approaching retirement and genuinely need to reduce risk.
2. If your life circumstances or financial goals have significantly changed.
3. If one asset has grown to dominate your portfolio to an extreme degree (we're talking 90%+ here). If that's happened, it's probably been an incredible run!

But for most people, most of the time? Let it ride.

Growth Over Balance

Here's the takeaway: don't let the pursuit of the perfect balance hold you back from maximum growth. If you're in it for the long haul (and if you're investing, you should be), then embracing a bit of "imbalance" might be the key to supercharging your returns.

Remember, the goal of investing isn't to have the prettiest, most perfectly balanced portfolio. It's to grow your wealth. And sometimes, that means letting your winners run and not fretting about keeping everything in perfect proportion.

So the next time you're tempted to rebalance just because it's been a while or because your stock allocation has grown, take a breather. Ask yourself: am I doing this because it's truly necessary or because it's what I've always been told to do? In the world of investing, sometimes the best action is inaction. Let your portfolio grow wild and free.

37

Ignore Capital Gains and Taxes

The Tax Tail Wagging the Investment Dog

You probably know how high tax rates are. Tax strategy and planning is an entire discipline within personal finance. Taxes should be a key consideration in every investment move, right? No. In fact, obsessing over the tax implications of your investments might be sabotaging your financial future. Let's get specific. You should ignore capital gains when making investment decisions.

Now, the problem isn't taxes themselves – it's letting the fear of taxes drive your investment strategy. It's like refusing to take a raise because you'll be in a higher tax bracket. Spoiler alert: you'll still have more money in your pocket.

When Avoiding Taxes Costs You a Fortune

Let me tell you a story that still keeps me up at night. I once had a client – let's call him Mr. Moneybags – who struck gold with a stock pick. This tiny position grew to dominate his portfolio, representing a significant chunk of his net worth. But here's the kicker: he refused to sell because he was terrified of the tax bill.

I get it. Nobody likes paying taxes. But here's the thing: Mr. Moneybags was so focused on avoiding a six-figure tax bill that he risked a seven-figure portfolio. It's like refusing to cash a winning lottery ticket because you don't want to pay the taxes on it.

When Losing Money Feels Like Winning

On the flip side, I've seen clients celebrate losing money. Yes, you read that right. They watch their profitable positions turn to losses, then sell with a sigh of relief because "at least I don't have to pay taxes."

Let that sink in for a moment. They'd rather lose money than pay taxes on their profits. It's like burning down your house to avoid paying property taxes. Sure, you've eliminated the tax bill, but at what cost?

Profits Minus Taxes Still Equals Profits

Here's a radical idea: if you're paying taxes on investment gains, it means you've made money. Intellectually, we all know this. But somehow, this simple fact gets lost in the fog of tax anxiety.

Let's break it down. If you make a $100,000 profit and have to pay $20,000 in taxes, you're still $80,000 richer than you were before. That's $80,000 you can reinvest, spend, or use to build a shrine to the investing gods. You do you.

When Inaction Leads to Losses

Here's where it gets really interesting. When you refuse to sell an investment because of potential tax implications, you're not just risking that specific investment. You're also missing out on other opportunities.

Maybe there's another investment that could yield even higher returns. Or perhaps you need that money for a once-in-a-lifetime business opportunity. By letting taxes dictate your decisions, you're potentially leaving money on the table.

When Tax Fear Leads to Risky Portfolios

Remember Mr. Moneybags? His reluctance to sell his winning stock left him with a dangerously lopsided portfolio. It's like putting all your eggs in one basket, then refusing to move any eggs because you're worried about egg tax. This can happen, as I mentioned, when you don't rebalance. However, when it gets to an extreme, take some profits!

The Right Way to Think About Tax Management

Now, I'm not saying you should completely ignore taxes. Tax-loss harvesting at the end of the year can be a smart strategy. But it should be the cherry on top of your investment sundae, not the main ingredient.

The goal should be to maximize your after-tax returns, not minimize your tax bill. Sometimes, that means biting the bullet and paying taxes on your gains.

Embracing Taxes as a Sign of Success

Here's a mindset shift that could change your financial life: start celebrating your tax bills. I'm serious. A big tax bill means you've had a great year financially. It's like complaining about the cost of champagne at your victory party.

Imagine looking at your tax bill and thinking, "Wow, I made so much money this year that I get to pay the interest on my government's debt." It's a bit pessimistic but a healthier mindset than tax paranoia.

Thinking Beyond the Next Tax Season

Investment decisions should be based on your long-term financial goals, not next year's tax bill. Are you saving for retirement? A child's education? A superyacht?

Whatever your goals, make decisions that align with those objectives. If that means realizing some gains and paying some taxes along the way, so be it.

Profits Trump Tax Paranoia

Look, I get it. Taxes are complicated, often confusing, and never fun. But letting tax concerns drive your investment strategy is like letting the tail wag the dog. Actually, it's worse - it's like letting the flea on the tail of the dog steer your entire financial future.

Here's your new mantra: "I hope I pay a ton in taxes this year because that means I made a boatload of money."

Remember, the goal of investing isn't to pay the least in taxes. It's to build wealth over time. And sometimes, building wealth means paying taxes on your successes along the way.

So, the next time you're hesitating to make an investment move because of tax implications, consider the bigger picture. Are you making this decision because it's the best move for your overall financial health, or are you just trying to avoid taxes? After all, in the grand chess game of investing, sometimes you have to sacrifice a pawn (your tax bill) to win the game (financial freedom).

IX

Real Estate

Is your home really your biggest and most important asset? Let's challenge conventional wisdom about home ownership and explore alternative approaches to real estate. Your view of property ownership is about to be flipped on its head.

38

Live With Your Parents

Rethinking the Rush to Move Out

Let's start with a truth bomb. You know that burning desire to move out of your parents' house? It's not your idea. It's a societal expectation drilled into your head since old ladies started gossiping about unfortunate kids moving back in with their parents.

But this rush to independence might be the very thing holding you back from true financial freedom. It's time to challenge the notion that success means having your own place.

Your Secret Weapon

Imagine for a moment that you had an extra $1,000, $1,500, or even $2,000 in your pocket every single month. No, I'm not talking about a get-rich-quick scheme or a sketchy side hustle. I'm talking about the magic of living rent-free with your parents.

When my sister got married and was expecting her first child, she moved back into our parents' house. Was it glamorous? Nope. Was it a financial game-changer? You bet your bottom dollar it was.

By living rent-free, she and her husband were able to save money, prepare for their new arrival, and get a solid financial footing without the crushing weight of rent and utilities hanging over their heads.

Jumpstart Your Future

When I graduated college, I was about as broke as any human could be. I started working immediately but still found myself shelling out $400 a month for a garage apartment that was one step above camping and not entirely legal. I was paying another $150 a month for utilities.

Now, let's do some quick math. If I had been able to live with my parents for just two years, I would have saved over $13,000. That would've been a pretty nice head start on life. And that was about the cheapest rent I had ever heard of. Many of my friends were paying $900 a month for basic studio apartments.

Think about what you could do with an extra $13,000 to $21,000 in your twenties. That's a down payment on a house, a significant dent in your student loans, or a hefty investment that could grow into a small fortune by the time you retire.

Strengthening Bonds While Building Wealth

Living with your parents isn't just about saving money. It's an opportunity to strengthen family bonds, learn from their life experiences, and create memories that will last a lifetime.

Think about it: How often do adults wish they had spent more time with their parents? By living at home, you're getting quality time that many people would kill for.

Statistics say that 98% of all the time you'll spend with your parents will be before you turn 18. Maybe it's time to reverse that trend and take advantage of more opportunities to be with family.

Embrace the Parental Pad

Look, I get it. Living with your parents might not be the coolest thing in the world. But you know what really sucks? Being broke, stressed, and financially unstable well into your thirties because you rushed to prove your independence.

Living with your parents isn't admitting defeat - it's making a strategic decision to set yourself up for long-term success. It's choosing financial freedom over societal expectations.

So the next time someone gives you grief about still living at home, think about the growing bank account, investments, and bright financial future you're building. Because, at the end of the day, true independence comes from financial security, not from having your name on a lease.

39

Don't Buy A House

The American Dream or Scheme?

You've heard it all your life: "Renting is throwing money away." "A house is the best investment you can make." "Owning a home is the cornerstone of the American Dream." These platitudes are so ingrained in our collective psyche that questioning them feels almost sacrilegious. But here's the thing: what if everything you thought you knew about home ownership was built on a foundation as shaky as a house of cards?

When Dreams Become Nightmares

Let's start with a little story. Meet Margo, a successful marketing executive in her early 30s. Margo did everything "right" according to the conventional playbook. She saved diligently for years, scrimping and saving until she finally had enough for a down payment on her dream home. The day she got her keys, she felt on top of the world. Fast forward five years and Margo's dream has turned into a nightmare of unexpected costs, time-consuming maintenance, and the creeping realization that her "investment" isn't performing as she'd hoped.

What They Don't Tell You at the Open House

Margo's story isn't unique. In fact, it's playing out in households across America. So why do we keep falling for the homeownership myth? Part of it is cultural conditioning, but a big part is also a fundamental misunderstanding of what home ownership really entails.

Let's talk about those hidden costs that nobody mentions at housewarming parties. When Margo bought her home, she thought her mortgage payment would be it. Oh, how wrong she was. Property taxes crept up year after year, eating into her budget. Home insurance was another monthly bite. And don't even get her started on maintenance. That charming old Victorian? The leaking basement, crumbling foundation, and uneven floors needed to be addressed. It turned out to be a money pit, with one major repair following another.

Real Estate's Dirty Little Secret

But at least her house was a great investment, right? Well, not so fast. When we really crunch the numbers, the returns on real estate are often less impressive than we're led to believe. Sure, home values tend to go up over time, but so does everything else. When adjusted for inflation, home prices have barely outpaced inflation over the long term. Meanwhile, the stock market has been doing laps around real estate returns.

The Freedom to Adapt

And let's talk about liquidity for a moment. Margo's friend Tom, who chose to rent and invest the difference, can easily sell off a portion of his stock portfolio if he needs quick cash. Margo, on the other hand, can't exactly sell off her guest bathroom when she's in a financial pinch.

Building Wealth or Building Chains?

Now, I can hear the homeownership advocates revving up their arguments. "But what about building equity?" they cry. "Renters have nothing to show for their monthly payments!" That is a fair point, but let's dig a little deeper. When you're paying a mortgage, especially in the early years, a huge chunk of your payment is going towards interest, not equity. And don't forget about all those other costs we mentioned earlier. By the time you factor those in, the equity you're building often looks a lot less impressive.

The Exceptions to the Rule

Now, I'm not saying that buying a home is always a bad idea. For some people, in some circumstances, it can make sense. If you're certain you want to stay in one place for a very long time, if you derive immense personal satisfaction from homeownership, or if you're in one of those rare markets where buying is significantly cheaper than renting, then by all means, go for it. But go into it with your eyes wide open, fully aware of the financial implications.

What Freedom Really Looks Like

For many of us, though, it might be time to redefine the American Dream. Instead of being tied down to a mortgage, what if our dream was financial freedom? The ability to live and work from anywhere in the world? A robust investment portfolio that isn't tied up in a single, illiquid asset? Weekends spent enjoying life, not mowing lawns and fixing gutters?

Making Decisions That Align With Your Values

Would you do something for me? Take a moment and really think about what you want from life. Is it the picket fence and the 30-year mortgage? Or is it the freedom to chase opportunities wherever they may lead? There's no right or wrong answer, but the important thing is that you're making a choice based on your own goals and values, not on what society tells you you're supposed to want.

Remember, the smartest financial decision isn't always the one that everyone else is making. It's the one that aligns with your desires for life and financial reality.

40

Always Get The Extended Warranty

Perspective on Home Warranties

I suckered you in a bit with this title. Extended warranties conjure up images of being pitched additional coverage at the checkout line in an electronics store. I never do that. If my electronics stop working, I'm coming back and complaining. However, when it comes to home warranties, I don't care who you are. You should have one. Experts hate them and typically recommend budgeting a percentage of your home's value for annual maintenance and repairs. However, conventional wisdom is outdated and flawed.

Let's examine the typical expert advice: "Set aside 1-4% of your home's value each year for maintenance and repairs." On the surface, this seems reasonable. However, this approach has some significant drawbacks.

Firstly, it assumes every homeowner will have an average experience. In reality, home repair needs can vary dramatically. Some homeowners might go years with minimal issues, while others face a series of major repairs in quick succession.

Secondly, when purchasing a home, especially an older one, you're often dealing with systems and appliances of unknown age and condition. The HVAC system or water heater could be on the verge of failure, and the potential repair or replacement costs could far exceed the suggested 1-4% budget.

Lastly, many people find themselves in a "house-rich, cash-poor" situation after buying a home. Buyers often spend their cash reserves on the down payment or fees for their dream house. After moving into their biggest asset, many homeowners ironically find themselves without access to cash and in a vulnerable position if a costly, unexpected expense were to pop up.

It's also worth noting that we regularly insure other aspects of our lives - cars, health, even phones. Yet when it comes to guaranteed repairs and maintenance on homes, often our largest investment, we're expected to self-insure. This approach seems inconsistent with our general attitude towards risk management.

Consider this: would most homeowners prefer guaranteed annual maintenance and repair coverage with a cap on out-of-pocket expenses, or would they rather hope they've saved enough to cover potential major repairs? The reality is that many homeowners aren't budgeting enough for expected maintenance, let alone preparing for worst-case scenarios.

The Financial Protection of Home Warranties

Now, let's challenge the notion that home warranties are just another unnecessary expense. When your AC fails during a heatwave, or your refrigerator stops working, the cost of repairs or replacement can be substantial. A home warranty offers a way to manage these expenses with a predictable monthly or annual fee.

Instead of facing unexpected four-figure (or five-figure) bills for major system or appliance failures, you're paying a set amount for coverage. When something breaks down, you're typically only responsible for a service call fee, which is usually a fraction of the full cost of repairs or replacement.

My Home Warranty Experience

I can speak to the benefits of home warranties from personal experience. I have warranties on both my primary residence and my investment property (about $40 a month for each), and they've proven to be valuable assets.

These warranties have covered the replacement of home systems and appliances that I never expected to fail so soon. As a landlord, they've simplified my property management significantly. When a tenant reports an issue, like a malfunctioning dishwasher, the warranty company deals directly with them. They handle the entire repair process, and I'm only responsible for the deductible (about $100). It's streamlined my role as a landlord and reduced my stress levels considerably.

The most surprising aspect has been the frequency of use. These warranties have paid for far more repairs than I anticipated. From minor fixes (electrical wiring and dishwasher repairs) to major replacements (both a furnace and an air conditioner replacement), the value I've received has far outweighed the cost of the warranties. I have peace of mind knowing that when something goes wrong, it's only going to cost me a few dollars, regardless of what it is.

Protection for Aging Homes

For those with older homes, a home warranty can be particularly beneficial. Older houses often come with older systems (like boilers) and appliances, which are more prone to breakdowns. A warranty can help manage the higher risk of repairs and replacements in these homes.

Instead of worrying about when the next major system might fail, you can have confidence knowing that you're covered. This can transform the experience of owning an older home from one of constant fear to one of enjoyment.

Budgeting Made Easier

One of the key advantages of a home warranty is the predictability it brings to home maintenance costs and your budget. Instead of guessing at potential repair expenses each month, you know exactly what you're spending on coverage. Instead of needing to sock away thousands of dollars in savings, it's just one less thing you have to worry about.

This predictability can be especially valuable in the often unpredictable world of homeownership, where the strangest things can happen. A warranty allows for more accurate financial planning and can help prevent the depletion of your emergency funds.

Time-Saving Benefits

Home warranties can save you considerable time and effort. When something breaks down, you don't need to spend hours researching repair companies, getting quotes, and coordinating service calls.

The warranty company typically has a network of pre-screened service providers. You make one call to the warranty company, and they handle the rest. This can be especially valuable for busy homeowners or those who aren't comfortable coordinating repairs themselves.

Quality Assurance

Home warranty companies often work with a network of licensed and insured professionals. This can provide an additional layer of quality assurance for repairs.

You're not just getting someone to fix the problem; you're getting a professional who meets the warranty company's standards. This can lead to higher-quality repairs and potentially longer-lasting solutions.

Long-Term Financial Strategy

While the monthly cost of a home warranty might seem like an added expense, it's important to consider the long-term financial implications. Over time, the money saved on repairs and replacements can significantly outweigh the warranty cost.

It's a form of financial protection against the unpredictable nature of home repairs. By managing these costs more effectively, you may be able to allocate more resources to other financial goals or investments.

A New Perspective on Home Protection

Home warranties offer a different approach to managing the costs and risks associated with home ownership. While they may not be the right choice for everyone, they deserve serious consideration, especially for those who value predictability and peace of mind.

Before dismissing home warranties based on conventional wisdom, take the time to evaluate your specific situation. Consider factors like the age of your home, the condition of your systems and appliances, your comfort with handling repairs, and your financial risk tolerance.

Remember, the smartest financial moves are often those that provide both practical benefits and peace of mind. A home warranty might just be that perfect blend of financial protection and stress relief for many homeowners.

X

Retirement

The traditional vision of retirement might be robbing you of life's joys. Let's explore radical new approaches to your golden years that prioritize living well now. Get ready to redefine what retirement means to you.

41

Ignore Account Contribution Limits

Unmasking the True Nature of Contribution Limits

Let's drop another truth bomb that might suddenly make your saving effort feel inadequate. Those retirement account contribution limits you've been religiously adhering to are totally irrelevant to your financial future.

Yep. The limits on your 401(k), IRA, or other retirement accounts aren't some carefully calculated threshold for your financial security. They're arbitrary numbers set by the government, designed to protect the government from losing too much tax revenue.

Why "Maxing Out" Isn't the Peak of Retirement Planning

Here's a phrase that makes me want to pull my hair out: "I'm maxing out my retirement accounts." It's usually said with a smug smile as if they've just snagged the gold medal of personal finance.

But here's the kicker: maxing out your accounts doesn't necessarily mean you're on track for a comfortable retirement. It's like hiking the trail when you're aiming for the summit. You may still have a long way to go.

Why Starting Late Means Limits Don't Apply

Let's do a little thought experiment. Imagine you started maxing out your retirement accounts at age 18. If you did that (I'd like to know what kind of job you were crushing at 18), you might be on track for a cushy retirement.

But for most of us mere mortals, our 20s and 30s were more about scraping together rent than maxing out 401(k)s. By the time we're earning enough to hit those contribution limits, we're playing a game of catch-up.

Why One Size Doesn't Fit All

Here's another inconvenient truth: those contribution limits don't know you. They don't know if you plan to retire to a quiet life of gardening and Netflix or if you're dreaming of sailing around the world on your yacht, enjoying prestige worldwide.

Your retirement needs are as unique as your fingerprint. Relying on generic contribution limits to determine your savings strategy is like using a one-size-fits-all hat to cover every head shape. Spoiler alert: it may not be enough.

Crunching the Real Numbers

So, how do you figure out what you really need? It's time to get cozy with some retirement calculators. They can help you estimate how much you'll need in retirement based on your desired lifestyle.

And here's where it gets interesting. You might find out you need to save way more than those contribution limits allow. Or, in some cases, you might not need to hit those limits at all. The point is, you won't know until you do the math.

Why Time is Your Greatest Asset

Here's a sobering thought: if you're only starting to max out your contributions in your 40s or 50s, you're likely way behind where you need to be. Those early years of compound interest are like rocket fuel for your retirement savings.

This is why it's crucial to start saving early, even if you can't hit the maximum. A smaller amount saved consistently from your 20s can outpace larger contributions started later in life.

When Limits Become Irrelevant

So, what if you find out you need to save more than the limits allow? Don't panic. This is where thinking outside the 401(k) box comes in handy.

Consider opening a non-qualified brokerage account. Yes, you'll miss out on some immediate tax advantages, but you'll have the freedom to save as much as you need. Or look into tax-sheltered options like annuities or even certain types of life insurance.

The key is not to let arbitrary limits dictate your financial future. Your retirement savings strategy should be based on your needs, not on some number dreamed up by bureaucrats.

Why Limits Can Lull You Into Complacency

Perhaps the biggest danger of these contribution limits is the false sense of security they provide. It's easy to think, "I'm maxing out my accounts, so I must be doing great!"

But this complacency can be a retirement killer. It might prevent you from reassessing your financial situation, exploring other investment opportunities, or making necessary lifestyle adjustments.

Your Retirement, Your Rules

Look, I get it. Maxing out your retirement accounts feels good. It's a very specific threshold, and achieving it can give you a sense of financial accomplishment. But don't let it be the end of your retirement planning journey.

Your retirement savings strategy should be as unique as you are. It should be based on your goals, your timeline, and your vision for the future. Don't let arbitrary limits set by the government dictate your financial destiny.

After all, your golden years should be about living your dreams. So ignore those limits, do your own math, and save what you need to make your retirement dreams a reality.

42

Don't Save In Retirement Accounts

The Siren Song of Tax-Deferred Savings

Let's start with a statement that usually raises every income tax red flag: you should stop saving exclusively in retirement accounts. Yes, the hallowed 401(k)s and IRAs may not be the most efficient way to hang onto most of your money.

Now, retirement accounts aren't bad. They're like that honor student in high school - impressive on paper but not necessarily the best at everything.

Deferring Isn't Always Preferring

Let's talk taxes. Traditional retirement accounts are like a financial time machine - they let you send your tax bill to the future. Sounds great!

But here's the catch: when you start withdrawing in retirement, Uncle Sam comes knocking. And he's not asking for the taxes on the money you contributed back then. He wants a cut of every single penny, including all that growth. It's like being penalized for your good investment choices. And since it avoided income tax once, it's going to get taxed at the income tax rate then - typically the highest rate on the tax food chain.

Flexing Your Financial Muscles

Enter the unappreciated hero of the investment world: the humble brokerage account. It's like the Swiss Army knife of investing - versatile, accessible, and surprisingly powerful.

With a brokerage account, you're not locked into contribution limits. You're not forced to wait until a certain age to access your money without penalty. And best of all, you're in control of your tax destiny.

Playing the Long Game for Lower Taxes

Here's where it gets really interesting. When you invest in a brokerage account, you're potentially setting yourself up for lower taxes in the long run.

How? Two words: capital gains. Capital gains tax rates can vary depending on your income and how long you've held the investment, but they're generally lower than ordinary income tax rates. For example, while your income might be taxed at 22% or 24%, long-term capital gains could be taxed at 0%, 15%, or 20%, depending on your total income.

Your Money, Your Rules

Let's face it: life is unpredictable. Maybe you'll want to retire early. Maybe you'll need to access your funds for an emergency. With a retirement account, you're often stuck until you hit that magic age of 59½ (unless you use the Substantially Equal Periodic Payments provision).

A brokerage account? It's like having a financial free agent. Need to pull some money out for a down payment on a house? Go for it. Want to start a business? Your funds are available for you.

Spreading Your Eggs Across Multiple Baskets

Now, I'm not saying you should abandon retirement accounts entirely. They're still a valuable tool in your financial arsenal. But relying on them exclusively is like trying to build a house with just a hammer. Sure, you can do it, but why would you when you have a full toolbox at your disposal?

By diversifying across retirement and non-retirement accounts, you're giving yourself options. You're creating a financial portfolio that is more tax-diverse and can adapt to whatever life throws your way.

Crunching the Numbers

Let's get down to brass tacks with some real numbers. This is where the rubber meets the road.

Larry puts $10,000 a year into a traditional 401(k) for 30 years, earning an average 7% return. At retirement, he has about $1,010,730. Sounds pretty good!

Now, let's look at Balki. He puts the same $10,000 a year into a brokerage account, also earning 7%. But here's where it gets interesting. He pays some capital gains taxes along the way, let's say 15% on the gains each year. This reduces his annual return to about 6.45%. After 30 years, he has $904,731.

"Aha!" you might say. "Larry still has more!" But we're not done yet. When Balki starts withdrawing, he only pays capital gains tax on the growth, not the principal. His total contributions were $300,000 (30 years x $10,000), so his taxable growth is $604,731. Assuming a 15% capital gains tax rate, he'll pay $90,710 in taxes.

But hold on! When Larry starts withdrawing from his 401(k), every dollar is taxed as income. Assuming a 22% tax bracket in retirement, his after-tax nest egg is really worth $788,369.

The result? Balki ends up with $814,021 after taxes, compared to Larry's $788,369. That's a difference of $25,652 in Balki's favor, or about $1,283 extra per year over 20 years of retirement - not exactly chump change.

Now, this is a simple comparison. There are many factors to consider, such as employer matching contributions and the net earned income to fund the brokerage account. However, the point is that conventional wisdom assumes that you take a tax advantage now and kick the tax can down the road. Without looking at your options, you may be giving up money.

And here's another issue: this example assumes tax rates stay the same. If income tax rates go up in the future (and let's face it, with the national debt, that's not a far-fetched idea), the brokerage account advantage could be even more significant.

The Power of Accessibility

Here's something the financial textbooks won't tell you. There's a psychological and practical benefit to having accessible funds, especially if you're aiming for early retirement. Knowing you can tap into your investments if needed provides a sense of security and control, and it's often essential for making early retirement a reality.

Traditional retirement accounts come with age restrictions that can handcuff early retirees. Want to retire at 45? This is where a brokerage account becomes your secret weapon. It offers the flexibility to fund your lifestyle before you hit the magical age of 59½, bridging the gap between early retirement and when you can access your tax-advantaged accounts penalty-free.

This isn't just feel-good fluff. It can lead to better financial decisions and open up more life options. When you're not feeling trapped by your savings strategy or arbitrary age limits, you're more likely to make rational, long-term choices. You might even find the courage to leave a soul-crushing job earlier than you thought possible, knowing you have accessible funds to support your transition to early retirement or a more fulfilling career.

Balancing Act for Maximum Benefit

Look, I'm not telling you to stop funding your 401(k) tomorrow. What I am saying is this: don't put all your financial eggs in the retirement account basket.

Consider this approach:

1. Contribute enough to your 401(k) to get any employer match. That's free money, after all.
2. Max out a Roth IRA if you're eligible. Tax-free growth is still a beautiful thing.
3. Then, direct additional savings into other accounts you may be overlooking, like a Health Savings Account or Employee Stock Purchase Plan. But definitely consider a brokerage account.

This strategy gives you the best of both worlds: tax advantages where they make sense and flexibility where you need it.

Remember, the goal isn't just to have the biggest retirement account but the one that will net you the most. It's also important to have the ones that give you financial freedom and security throughout your life and into retirement.

So go ahead, check out a brokerage account, and maybe start coloring outside the retirement account lines.

43

Don't Use The Stock Market For Retirement Income

The Conventional Wisdom Trap

You've heard this advice before. Save diligently, invest in the stock market, watch your nest egg grow, and then withdraw 4% annually to retire. It's a mantra repeated by financial advisors, money gurus, and probably anyone who's saved some money. But what if I told you this conventional wisdom might be limiting your potential for a truly secure and fulfilling retirement?

Don't get me wrong – the stock market can be a powerful tool for wealth accumulation. But treating it as the only option for retirement income is ignoring some options that might be more flexible, more lucrative, and even more secure.

Exploring Alternative Retirement Strategies

Let's face it: relying solely on the stock market for your golden years is a bit like putting all your eggs in one very volatile basket. Market crashes, economic downturns, and unforeseen global events can wreak havoc on your carefully planned portfolio. So, what's a savvy soon-to-be retiree to do?

The Annuity Advantage

Enter annuities with guaranteed lifetime withdrawal benefits. These financial products can offer a safety net that the stock market simply can't match. Imagine locking in your gains and saying goodbye to those stomach-churning market dips. Some annuities even let you participate in market upswings while protecting you from the downside. It's like having your cake and eating it too – with a side of financial security for dessert.

Thinking Outside the Stock Box

But why stop there? As a zig-zag thinker (yes, that's still a compliment), you have the power to see opportunities where others see dead ends. Your retirement plan doesn't have to be a one-size-fits-all solution. Let's explore some unconventional yet potentially lucrative alternatives:

1. **The Accidental Landlord**: Picture this – instead of withdrawing from a dwindling stock portfolio, you're collecting rent checks from a multi-unit residential building. That's exactly what one couple did with $800,000, securing a steady income stream and a tangible asset that could appreciate over time. Who says you can't be a real estate mogul in retirement?
2. **The Business Buyer**: Ever dreamed of being your own boss? One retiree invested seven figures into an established business, leveraging his industry expertise to grow the company and generate more income than his former day job – all while working on his own terms. It's not just about passive income; it's about creating a legacy.
3. **The Niche Market Navigator**: From rebranding a small gym to target high-end clients, to turning a vacant lot into a trucker's paradise for trailer storage, thinking creatively can turn modest investments into reliable income streams. The key is identifying underserved markets and meeting their needs.
4. **The Car Wash King**: Who knew that helping people keep their cars clean

could pave the way to financial freedom? One enterprising retiree built a mini-empire of self-service car washes, proving that sometimes the simplest ideas can yield the most satisfying results.
5. **The Mobile Home Maestro**: By purchasing and upgrading a mobile home park, another retiree not only secured a steady income but also created a desirable community, proving that improving lives can go hand-in-hand with improving your financial situation.
6. **The Digital Domain Dynamo**: In our increasingly online world, buying and optimizing e-commerce stores and digital businesses can be a low-overhead, high-return strategy. One savvy retiree turned his marketing know-how into a six-figure income by breathing new life into underperforming online ventures.

Redefining Retirement Success

The beauty of these alternative strategies isn't just in their potential for higher returns. It's about creating income streams that can sustain your lifestyle indefinitely, rather than watching your savings dwindle year after year.

By thinking creatively, you might find that you need less capital than you thought to achieve your retirement goals. Imagine deploying just a fraction of your assets to secure a core income stream while keeping the rest as a safety net or for future ventures.

The Zig-Zag Path to Financial Freedom

Embracing these unconventional approaches doesn't mean abandoning traditional investments entirely. It's about expanding your horizons and creating a diversified strategy that works for you. By combining the stability of some conventional methods with the potential of alternative investments, you can build a retirement plan that's not just about surviving but thriving.

Remember, the goal isn't to follow a prescribed path to retirement. It's about creating a lifestyle that brings you joy, security, and perhaps even a new sense of purpose. Whether that means becoming a part-time entrepreneur, a real estate investor, or finding your own unique niche, the possibilities are limited only by your imagination.

44

Have A Mortgage In Retirement

Debunking Retirement's Golden Rule

Let's rethink how we feel about some debt. Specifically, I think you should have a mortgage in retirement. Carrying debt into your golden years might be the smartest move.

Now, the conventional wisdom of entering retirement with a paid-off home is based on old strategies that simply don't hold up for many of today's retirees.

When Savings Fall Short

Here's a hard truth: most people are woefully underprepared for retirement. The average retirement savings wouldn't fund a Disney vacation, let alone fund the globe-trotting, bucket-list-crushing retirement you've been dreaming about.

So, what if I told you there was a way to turn your biggest asset - your home - into a source of income rather than just a paid-off piece of property?

Turning Your Home into an ATM

Enter the reverse mortgage. It's not just for late-night infomercials anymore. For homeowners 62 and older, a reverse mortgage can be a financial lifeline, allowing you to tap into your home equity without selling or moving.

Imagine this: you get to stay in your home, you stop making mortgage payments, and you receive a steady stream of income. It's like your house is finally paying you back for all those years of mortgage payments.

Liberating Your Retirement Income

Here's where it gets really interesting. By eliminating your mortgage payment, you're freeing up a significant chunk of your monthly income. For many retirees, this could mean the difference between scraping by and living comfortably.

Think about it. If your mortgage was eating up 30-50% of your income during your working years, what would happen if that expense suddenly disappeared? Even if you never borrowed another cent from your home, just turning off the monthly mortgage obligation could be a game changer. Suddenly, that fixed income doesn't seem so limiting, does it?

Funding Your Bucket List

Let's talk about that bucket list of yours. You know, the one gathering dust while you worry about making ends meet? A reverse mortgage could be your ticket to making those dreams a reality.

Maybe it's that trip to Paris you've always wanted to take or the vintage car you've been eyeing. With the extra income from a reverse mortgage, these don't have to remain pipe dreams. You could be sipping champagne on the Champs-Élysées instead of drinking Folgers Crystals at your kitchen table.

Tailoring Your Mortgage to Your Needs

One size doesn't fit all, especially when it comes to retirement planning. A reverse mortgage gives you options. You can take the money as a lump sum, a line of credit, or as monthly payments. It's like having a flexible tool in your retirement toolbox.

And here's the kicker: the unused portion of your line of credit actually grows over time. It's like having a savings account that you don't have to fund.

Balancing Your Needs with Your Heirs'

Now, I know what some of you are thinking: "But what about leaving something for the kids?" Let me ask you this: would your kids rather inherit a paid-off house or have vibrant, fulfilled parents?

If you're lucky enough to have thoughtful children (and I hope you are), they'll want you to enjoy your retirement to the fullest. As someone who hopes his own parents live it up in their golden years, I can tell you that the greatest gift you can give your kids is the example of a life without regrets.

Leveraging Real Estate Trends

Here's a little-known benefit of keeping a mortgage: it allows you to take advantage of real estate market trends. If property values in your area are on the rise, your home equity grows even as you tap into it.

Rethinking Retirement Finance

Look, I know what people are going to say. The idea of carrying debt into retirement goes against everything we've been taught, or it's just a tool for poor people. But in a world where pensions are disappearing and Social Security is uncertain, we need to rethink our approach to retirement finance.

A mortgage - whether traditional or reverse - can be a powerful tool in your retirement arsenal. It can provide financial flexibility, fund your dreams, and, yes, even offer peace of mind.

So, before you rush to pay off your mortgage before retirement, take a step back. Consider your full financial picture. Think about what you want your retirement to look like. And don't be afraid to buck conventional wisdom if it means living the retirement you've always dreamed of.

Remember, the goal of retirement planning isn't to die with the most assets. It's to live your best life with the resources you have. And if that means keeping a mortgage, well, that might just be the smartest financial move you ever make.

After all, you can't take it with you - but with a well-planned mortgage strategy, you can sure enjoy it while you're here.

45

Don't Retire In America

The Great American Retirement Myth

Ah, retirement! If you do everything right, you get one of your own. Work hard, save diligently, and retire comfortably in the good ol' US of A. It's a nice story, isn't it? But what if I told you that your golden years could be not just comfortable but downright luxurious - if you're willing to think outside the borders?

It's time to consider the unthinkable: retiring outside the United States. Before you start raising your flag in protest, think about it. This might just be the most financially savvy move you'll ever make.

Your Ticket to Financial Freedom

Let's talk about a fancy term that could change your life: geoarbitrage. No, it's not highly technical. It's the practice of taking your hard-earned dollars to a place where they stretch further than you ever thought possible.

But before we jet off to exotic locales, let's crunch some numbers closer to home. Imagine this: you've hit the ripe age of 67, ready to retire, but your nest egg is more nest than egg. You've got $60,000 in your retirement account. In the US, that's barely enough to keep you in coffee and crossword puzzles.

Let's break it down:

With an annual return of 5%, you could safely withdraw about $300 a month to make sure your money lasts. Add in the average Social Security benefit for a 67-year-old retired worker - $1,883.50 as of 2023 - and you're looking at a grand total of $2,183.50 per month.

In many parts of the US, that's a one-way ticket to beans and rice. You'd be pinching pennies, clipping coupons, and saying goodbye to any dreams of a comfortable retirement.

But here's where geoarbitrage works its magic. Take that same $2,183.50 and hop on a plane to Chiang Mai, Thailand. Suddenly, you're not just surviving - you're thriving.

In Chiang Mai, here's what your "meager" US retirement funds could get you:

- **A spacious, modern apartment in a desirable area**: $500/month
- **Utilities, including high-speed internet**: $70/month
- **Delicious meals out**: $400/month
- **Health insurance**: $100/month
- **Transportation** (motorbike rental or plenty of taxi rides): $100/month
- **Entertainment, including movies, massages, and cultural activities**: $200/month
- **Total**: $1,370/month

That leaves you with over $800 for savings, travel, or extra indulgences. Want a maid to clean your apartment twice a week? That'll be about $100/month. Fancy a weekend trip to a nearby island? Easy peasy.

In the US, your $2,183.50 might have you choosing between medication and meals. In Chiang Mai, it has you choosing between a sunset cocktail on your balcony or a spa day.

And Chiang Mai is just one example. Consider this:

- **Cuenca, Ecuador**: a couple can live comfortably on $1,500-$1,800 per

month.
- **Penang, Malaysia**: $2,000 a month will get you a lifestyle that would cost $4,000-$5,000 in most US cities.
- **Lagos, Portugal**: $2,200 a month can fund a Mediterranean lifestyle that would be the envy of your US-based friends.
- **Da Nang, Vietnam**: A coastal city with modern amenities where $1,500-$2,000 a month covers rent, food, and entertainment, giving you a beachfront lifestyle.
- **Cebu City, Philippines:** Known as the "Queen City of the South," Cebu offers a mix of urban convenience and island life. A budget of $1,500-$2,000 per month would cover rent, utilities, food, and entertainment, giving you access to beaches, resorts, and a vibrant city life.
- **Budapest, Hungary**: With $2,000 a month, you can live in a historic European city with excellent healthcare, great public transport, and a lower cost of living than Western Europe.
- **Playa del Carmen, Mexico**: A couple can live a comfortable, beach-centered lifestyle for about $2,000-$2,400 per month, which includes rent, utilities, and entertainment.
- **Bucharest, Romania:** A historic city where $2,000 a month can provide a comfortable lifestyle, including modern apartments and rich cultural experiences.
- **Sofia, Bulgaria**: Known for its affordability, a budget of $1,500-$2,000 can get you a great lifestyle with access to mountains, history, and low living costs.
- **Krakow, Poland**: For $2,000 a month, you can enjoy a high standard of living in this culturally rich city, including affordable rent, food, and transportation.

It's like getting a massive raise just for packing your bags. When was the last time relocating got you a lifestyle upgrade like that?

The Social Security Jackpot

"But what about my Social Security?" I hear you ask. Well, here's a little-known secret: Uncle Sam is cool with you taking your Social Security check abroad. In fact, in some countries, it might feel like you've hit the jackpot.

Thanks to favorable exchange rates, your monthly check could go from "barely covering groceries" to "living it up on the beach." It's like getting a raise for moving. When was the last time relocating got you a pay bump?

The Tax Man Cometh Not

Here's something that might make you do a double-take: the Foreign Earned Income Exclusion. In plain English? If you're living abroad, you might be able to exclude a significant chunk of your income from U.S. taxes.

In 2023, that exclusion is up to $120,000 per person. Uncle Sam might let you keep more of your hard-earned cash if you're soaking up the sun on a foreign beach. It's like getting a "thank you" note from the IRS. That's as rare as hen's teeth.

The Healthcare Vacation

Now, I know what you're thinking. "But what about healthcare? I've heard horror stories!" Well, prepare to have your mind blown. Many countries offer high-quality healthcare at a fraction of the cost in the U.S.

In Mexico, you could see a specialist for $30-$40. A dental crown that would cost $1,000 in the U.S. might set you back $250 in Costa Rica. And in Thailand, you might find yourself in a hospital that feels more like a five-star hotel. It's like going on vacation and coming back with a new hip and a tan.

The Climate Control

Let's face it: the weather in much of the U.S. is about as predictable as a cat's mood. One day, you're shoveling snow; the next, you're melting on the sidewalk. But what if you could choose your perfect climate?

Want eternal spring? Try Ecuador. Prefer a tropical paradise? Thailand's got you covered. Fancy a Mediterranean climate? Portugal is calling your name. It's like having a weather remote control.

The Adventure of a Lifetime

Retirement doesn't have to mean rocking chairs and early bird specials. It can be the beginning of your greatest adventure. Are you already dreaming of seeing the world during vacation? Why make it just a brief two-week vacation that'll drain your budget? Stay longer and spend less as a long-term visitor. Imagine waking up to the sound of howler monkeys in Costa Rica or sipping espresso in an Italian piazza.

Every day is an opportunity to learn something new, taste exotic flavors, and make friends from around the world. It's like being a college student again, minus the exams and stress.

Your Home Away From Home

Worried about making friends? Don't be. Popular retirement destinations are teeming with expat communities. From book clubs in Buenos Aires to golf leagues in Phuket, you'll find your tribe. And the best part? Everyone's in the same boat, eager to make friends and explore their new home. It's like a ready-made social network, just waiting for you to plug in.

The Family Ties That Bind (Across Oceans)

"But what about my family?" I hear you ask. Well, let me ask you this: how often do you really see your adult children now? Remember that statistic that says 98% of the time a parent spends with their child happens before age 18. It makes you think, doesn't it?

But here's the silver lining: when you live in an exotic location, family may be more likely to visit and stay longer. Your grandkids won't just be coming over for Sunday dinner; they'll be having the adventure of a lifetime with you in your adopted country. Plus, with today's technology, you're never more than a video call away. It's like having your family in the next room, except the "room" is a beautiful beach in Bali.

Your Retirement, Supercharged

Look, I'm not saying retiring abroad is for everyone. It comes with its challenges - language barriers, cultural differences, figuring out how to say "Where's the bathroom?" in another language (although there's some universal sign language).

But if you're willing to take the leap, retiring abroad can transform your golden years from a financial tightrope walk into a luxury experience. Your dollars can stretch further, your adventures can be grander, and your retirement can be, well, simply more.

And here's the beauty of geoarbitrage: if you've had your fill of one place, you can simply move on to another. You're not obligated to live anywhere forever. This flexibility allows you to experience various cultures, climates, and lifestyles throughout your retirement years.

So before you resign yourself to a retirement of clipping coupons and watching the Weather Channel, consider an international upgrade. Your perfect retirement might be waiting for you, just a passport stamp away. Remember, retirement isn't just about having enough to live. It's about having the freedom to truly live. So pack your bags, grab your sense of adventure, and get ready for the retirement of a lifetime. The world is waiting.

46

End With Nothing

When Saving Becomes Hoarding

Let's start with an idea that's going to trigger your selfless side: you should aim to die with zero dollars. The concept of retirement is often wrapped up in fear. There's always a problem saving enough for retirement. There's a problem managing it to last long enough. There's the risk of living too long. There's an obsession with preserving the principal indefinitely, so you're not homeless on the street during your final days.

Maximizing Experiences, Minimizing Regrets

Here's the cold, hard truth: you can't take it with you. Yet, so many of us plan our retirements as if we're packing for an eternal vacation. But let's face it, the only guaranteed journey we're taking is the one-way trip to the great beyond.

So why not make the most of the time you have? Every dollar you leave unspent is a potential experience unlived, a memory unmade, a moment of joy unrealized. It's time to start thinking of your savings not as a nest egg to be preserved but as a treasure chest to be emptied.

Your Taxpayer-Funded Backup Plan

Now, I know what you're thinking. "But what if I outlive my money?" Well, here's a comforting (or disturbing, depending on your political leanings) thought: if you make it to 95 and run out of cash, society's got your back.

Medicaid, social programs, and taxpayer-funded care facilities exist for a reason. Is it the lap of luxury? Probably not. But were you living in the lap of luxury up to that point? You might be more concerned with your daily Jell-O flavor than your investment portfolio's performance.

Why Your Kids Don't Need Your Money

Let's talk about the elephant (or children) in the room: leaving an inheritance. Many of us feel obligated to leave a financial legacy for our children. But here's a radical thought: maybe your kids don't expect or want anything from you. Maybe your kids only worry about you being able to support yourself. Maybe they're worried that you might be a financial burden to them. Maybe the best gift you can give your kids is the peace of mind that they won't have to help fund your retirement years.

As someone who's told his own parents to spend every dime of their money, I can attest that there's freedom in not expecting an inheritance. It pushes you to create your own financial success rather than waiting for a windfall that may never come. Plus, there's no way I could ever repay my parents for everything they've done for me. At the very least, I can happily encourage them to make the most of their own money.

Don't Wait Until It's Too Late

How many times have you put off a dream vacation, a luxury purchase, or a charitable donation because you're saving for "someday"? Well, newsflash: someday is now.

If you've spent your entire working life deferring gratification, when exactly do you plan to start enjoying the fruits of your labor? When you're too old to climb the steps of Machu Picchu? When your taste buds can no longer appreciate that fine wine you've been saving for?

It's time to give yourself permission to spend. You've earned it, literally.

Be Your Own Foundation

Here's a new spin on an old idea: instead of leaving a lump sum to your heirs or a charity after you're gone, why not become a living, breathing philanthropist?

Imagine the satisfaction of seeing your money make a difference in real-time. Whether it's funding your grandkid's education, volunteering for a cause you're passionate about, or just treating your loved ones to experiences they couldn't otherwise afford - the joy of time together is unparalleled.

When Caution Becomes Regret

Let's talk about risk for a moment. Traditional financial advice is all about minimizing risk. But have you considered that being too cautious might be the biggest risk of all?

The risk of reaching the end of your life with a fat bank account and a thin book of memories. The risk of realizing too late that you've been the proverbial donkey, always chasing the carrot of financial security without ever taking a bite.

Calculated Hedonism

Now, I'm not advocating for reckless abandon (at least not all of the time). The goal isn't to blow through your savings in your own Fyre Festival. What I'm proposing is calculated hedonism.

Start by estimating your life expectancy (morbid but necessary). Then, create a spending plan that aims to deplete your assets around that time (depending on your comfort level). Factor in potential health care costs, but also factor in those bucket list items you've been putting off.

Adjusting Course as You Go

One key to this approach is staying flexible. If the market takes a downturn, you can adjust your spending. If you find yourself with unexpected longevity, you can dial things back. The key is to remain engaged with your finances rather than setting them on autopilot and hoping for the best.

Freedom Through Spending

Here's a counterintuitive truth: there's immense freedom in planning to spend it all. No more worrying about preserving principal or maintaining a certain withdrawal rate. No more guilt about "dipping into savings."

Instead, you're free to focus on what really matters: making the most of every day you have left. Because at the end of the day (or life), the memories you've made and the impact you've had will be far more valuable than a number in a bank account.

Live Rich, Die Broke

Look, I get it. The idea of spending down your assets goes against most of what we've been taught about responsible financial planning. It feels risky, maybe even a little reckless.

But here's the thing: the biggest risk in life isn't running out of money. It's running out of time to do the things that matter most to you.

So, I challenge you to rethink your retirement strategy. Instead of aiming for a certain dollar amount, aim for a life rich in experiences, generosity, and joy. Plan your finances not just for longevity but also to make the most of the fleeting time you have. You can't take it with you, but you can sure as hell can enjoy it while you're here.

XI

Eyes Wide Open

Let's pull back the curtain on the personal finance industry. Prepare for some uncomfortable truths about the advice you've been sold, and discover a new path forward. Your awakening is almost complete.

47

The Truth They Don't Want You to Know

The Great Financial Illusion

As we reach the end of our journey together, it's time to pull back one giant curtain on the world of personal finance. Brace yourself because what you're about to learn might shake the very foundation of everything you thought you knew about money.

Remember all those golden rules of finance we've been fed over the years? Save diligently, invest in index funds, cut out the coffee, and someday off in the distant future, you'll be rich. I hate to break it to you, but we've been sold a bill of goods. The emperor of personal finance? He's not wearing any clothes.

The Outdated Playbook

Before we dive deeper into the world of financial advice, let's address two crucial realities that shape our financial landscape: the outdated nature of common financial rules and the vested interests that keep these rules in place.

Old Rules in a New Economy

Many of the financial commandments we've been taught are relics of a bygone era, stubbornly clinging to relevance in a rapidly changing economic landscape. Sure, some fundamentals of money management are timeless, but the devil's in the details - and boy, have those details changed.

Today's workers are navigating a financial obstacle course that would make their grandparents' heads spin. Defined benefit retirement plans? Most have gone the way of the dodo. Job security? It's as rare as a unicorn in today's gig economy. Meanwhile, costs are skyrocketing faster than SpaceX - we're talking housing, healthcare, education, you name it. Oh, and let's not forget about taxes, which seem to have an insatiable appetite for our paychecks. All this while income growth is elusive.

So, when we're fed the same old financial advice that worked wonders in the 1970s, it's like trying to fix a smartphone with a hammer and chisel. Sure, these tried-and-true money rules might still work... or they might be as useful as a dial-up modem in a Wi-Fi world.

The Entrenched System

Now, you might wonder why these outdated rules persist. The answer lies in the entrenched system that profits from maintaining the status quo. The established financial industry continues to spout the same advice because selling the same services and products is immensely profitable. If they don't have to spend money creating and marketing innovative products, their profit margins stay consistent and safe.

But it goes deeper than that. Many players in the system have a vested interest in keeping things exactly as they are:

- Financial institutions profit from traditional investment products and services.
- Gurus make millions selling books and seminars based on the same old advice.

- Governments rely on current retirement and tax systems to function.

Think about this. If everyone embraced side hustles, where's the profit for traditional employers? If masses of people retired overseas, it would threaten established domestic industries. If early retirement became the norm, social security systems could crumble.

The existing system has a lot of players - from gurus to financial institutions to governments - that don't want it to change. They're not incentivized to embrace or promote trends that could disrupt their comfortable status quo.

The Need for Zigzag Thinking

This is why we need to become better zigzag thinkers. The rules of the game are constantly shifting, and the ability to adapt and think creatively about your finances isn't just an advantage - it's a necessity.

Maybe these old rules need a 21st-century makeover. Perhaps they need to be tweaked, adjusted, or turned completely inside out. By questioning these age-old financial mantras and looking at them from new angles, you might just stumble upon that one disruptive idea that changes everything for you.

As we embark on this journey of financial myth-busting, keep your mind open and your thinking flexible. You'll need new tools and adaptable strategies to thrive in the current economy. Remember, the next unconventional idea could be your ticket to financial freedom in a world where the old rules no longer apply.

The Guru Conspiracy

Now, let's shine some light on the financial advice gurus. What I'm about to share is a world I've only fully decoded in recent years, and it might just blow your mind.

Years ago, I was just a cog in the machine of a giant financial services corporation, tasked with booking a big-name financial guru to headline our next client event. After scouring the landscape of fiscal celebrities, I landed on Penny Wiseman (obviously anonymized), the queen of the "Budget, Save, Invest" mantras.

Negotiations ensued, contracts were signed, and over the next few meetings, I got to know Penny as we prepared for the event. Her topics were straightforward: budget like a boss, save like there's no tomorrow, invest like Warren Buffett. It was exactly what our company embraced and taught itself. But as our professional relationship evolved, I started to get a peek behind the curtain.

One day, over a fancy lunch, I asked, "So, is there a particular concept you teach that really changed your life?"

"You know," she says, "none of these principles actually got me to financial independence."

Slightly surprised, I asked, "So what made the difference for you?"

She leaned in. "By teaching these principles, I built my own financial education empire. Books, TV appearances, speaking gigs - that's where the real money is."

As Penny continued, I realized I was getting a masterclass in irony. This guru of frugality didn't have a traditional job, a 401(k), or employer matching funds. What she had was a money-printing machine fueled by leaving the rat race and reinventing herself as a business owner.

That's when it hit me - the total disconnect between what these gurus were teaching and what they were actually doing in their own lives. They were preaching traditional financial strategies while they were using the latest techniques, creative approaches, and accelerated plans.

As I watched Penny prepare to go on stage, ready to dispense wisdom about pinching pennies to a crowd, I couldn't help but marvel at the absurdity of it all. Here was a woman who had truly mastered the art of making money - not by following the traditional advice but by setting it all aside. While advising others on how to achieve their dreams, she realized that the same approach wasn't good enough for her.

The Real Rules of the Game

Over the years, what I've discovered is both revealing and thought-provoking. Here's the truth about how financial gurus really play the game:

1. **The Seminar Circuit and Leverage**: Those inspirational seminars? They're cash cows. One guru confided that a single weekend could net him more than most people's annual salary. Instead of slowly saving a portion of their salaries, they focus on creating products and services that can be sold repeatedly with minimal additional effort.
2. **The Book Deal Bonanza and Personal Branding**: Publishing contracts with six-figure advances are common, turning financial advice into a bestselling industry. These gurus understand that in the digital age, a personal brand can be more valuable than any stock portfolio.
3. **The Sponsorship Shuffle and Multiple Income Streams**: Those picture-perfect Instagram posts of gurus living the high life? Often bankrolled by sponsors eager to reach their massive followings. While preaching the security of a steady job, they're busy diversifying their own income sources through various business ventures.
4. **The Business Behind the Advice and Strategic Partnerships**: The real money isn't about following their own advice - it's about building businesses around their personal brands. Online courses, coaching programs, affiliate marketing - the list goes on. Building relationships and collaborations often played a bigger role in their success than any 401(k) ever did.

So, while these gurus preach about pinching pennies and the magic of compound interest, they're playing a different game entirely. They're leveraging their knowledge and reputation to build empires, not nest eggs. It's not about slow and steady savings for them - it's about creating money-making machines that work even while they sleep.

Now that you've peeked behind the curtain, you're in on the game. But here's the kicker: you don't need a bestseller or a million followers to start thinking like them. Maybe you can find ways to leverage your skills at work or finally get that side hustle off the ground. It could even mean rethinking what "financial freedom" looks like for you. The point is, now that you've seen how the big dogs play, why not take a page from their book? After all, the best way to beat the game is to change how you play it. Welcome to the other side of financial advice - where the real money moves are made.

The Great Awakening

Now, I can almost hear you lamenting, "Great, so it's all a scam? What hope is there for the rest of us?" But here's where it gets exciting. This revelation isn't the end - it's just the beginning.

The truth is, the basic principles of personal finance - living below your means, investing for the long term, and being prepared for emergencies - are all still important (as my father likes to remind people). They're the foundation upon which financial success is built. You'll probably be fine if you do these consistently over your lifetime.

The real secret is figuring out "how" to do it. How do you keep your budget in balance if homes are unaffordable? How do you invest if you can't truly diversify? How do you retire if your accounts don't grow? True financial freedom comes from crafting your unique roadmap, even if it flies in the face of conventional wisdom.

Your Roadmap to Real Wealth

So, where do we go from here? How can you apply these insights to your own life? Here are some ideas to consider on your new roadmap to wealth:

1. **Embrace Your Inner Entrepreneur**: Look for opportunities to create value in scalable ways. Can your skills or knowledge be turned into a product or service?
2. **Build Your Personal Brand**: In today's digital world, your personal brand can be your most valuable asset. Start sharing your expertise,

whether through a blog, YouTube channel, podcast, or just becoming more invaluable at work.
3. **Diversify Your Income**: Don't rely on a single paycheck. Look for ways to create multiple streams of income, both active and passive.
4. **Invest in Yourself**: Use some of your savings to acquire new skills that can help you build businesses, advance your career, or bring you happiness.
5. **Network Strategically**: Sometimes, who you know is as important as what you know. Attend industry events, join professional associations, and build relationships with people who inspire you.
6. **Think Like a Business**: Even if you stay an employee, approach your career like a business. How can you increase your value to the market? How can you become a connector, an authority, or a leader?

The Contradiction Conundrum

Now, here's where it gets even more interesting. Throughout this book, you've probably noticed some advice that seems to contradict itself. For example, I said not to buy a house but then suggested getting a mortgage in retirement. I advocated for renting an apartment but also recommend living with your parents. Guess what? I'm fully aware of these contradictions, and that's precisely the point.

The world of personal finance is full of hard and fast rules that often conflict with each other. You've got financial experts screaming at you from every direction. "Save for retirement like your life depends on it!" they cry. But then they say, "Don't forget your kid's college fund!" And just when you think you've got it figured out, they hit you with, "Pay cash for that car, especially if you're drowning in debt!"

It's enough to make your head spin. However, by blindly accepting one side of an argument, you're never giving yourself a chance to evaluate an alternative.

Now, conventional wisdom says, "If multiple experts agree, it must be true!" After all, who are we mere mortals to question the almighty financial overlords? Swimming against this current of "expert" opinion is about as advisable as dipping your toes into a shark tank. It's so much cozier to nestle into the warm embrace of regurgitated financial platitudes than to venture into the cold, harsh waters of new ideas.

I want you to remember that the path to wealth is rarely a straight line and usually isn't obvious. It's time to embrace your inner zig-zag thinker and chart a course that's uniquely yours.

Yes, save and invest. Yes, be mindful of your spending. But don't stop there. That's why I want you to be willing to welcome contradictions and use them as inspiration to think critically. Question everything. Find your own answers. Every financial guru you admire started exactly where you are right now. The only difference? They decided to play the game according to their own rules.

Your Call to Action

So here's my challenge to you. Take what you've learned in this book and use it as a launching pad. Take action on something you know is right for you but hesitated because you were worried about the optics, the experts, or even society.

The world is waiting for what you have to offer. And who knows? A year from now, you might just be sharing your unique path to financial freedom. The game has changed, and now you know the real rules. Are you finally ready to play? Your unique expedition to true financial independence starts now.

About the Author

Peter Waitzman is the founder and CEO of Expedition Money LLC, an innovative financial wellness accelerator that delivers a broad spectrum of financial strategies in a fun and engaging style. He is an author, speaker, and financial wellness enthusiast with over two decades of professional experience in personal finance.

You can connect with me on:
- http://www.waitzman.com

Also by Peter Waitzman

I write books sharing the things I've discovered on my journey to improve my life because I want to help you discover your ideal life too.

Vacations Are A Need: Practical Tips To Make Extraordinary Memories Affordable
This is your ultimate guide to finding a refreshing trip while keeping your budget intact. This comprehensive resource is packed with ingenious travel hacks, insider tips, and practical advice to ensure you can enjoy extraordinary adventures without breaking the bank.

Be Discovered: How to Market Your Financial Coaching Business

Whether you're just starting out or looking to take your existing coaching practice to the next level, this book will give you the tools, strategies, and inspiration you need to succeed. Don't just be a financial coach – be discovered and **make a lasting difference** in the lives of your clients.

How To Get Out Of Debt Fast: Scratch, Claw, Strategize, & Shortcut

Getting out of debt does not have to mean a lifetime of sacrifices. Your journey could be shorter than you think. If you're ready to make the expedition to freedom as fast as possible, then start here.

Money Is Factscinating: Fascinating Money Facts, History, Stories & Trivia

Dive into the captivating world of money with "MONEY IS FACTSCINATING," a treasure trove of more than **100 entertaining, informative, and educational stories** that explore the many facets of currency. From mind-blowing tales and historical anecdotes to hilarious mishaps and cutting-edge financial technology, this book offers a fresh and engaging perspective on the subject that makes the world go round.

Amazing Money Stories: True Tales of Greed, Generosity, Success & Luck

Discover a treasure trove of astonishing true stories about money in "Amazing Money Stories: True Tales of Greed, Generosity, Success & Luck" by Peter Waitzman. This captivating collection unveils the incredible ways people have amassed fortunes, realized their wildest dreams, pulled off audacious scams, and uncovered mind-boggling facts about wealth.

The Accidental YouTuber: How I Make a Six-Figure Income on YouTube

In **The Accidental Youtuber**, embark on a journey with Peter as he shares his rollercoaster ride **from orphan to YouTube success**. With a blend of **candid storytelling** and actionable insights, this book unveils the secrets behind creating engaging content, growing a loyal audience, and monetizing your passion on the world's largest video platform.

Discovering Travel Bliss: Insider Secrets For Transforming Ordinary Trips Into Joyful Journeys

With insider tips and real-world examples, this book will equip you to create vacations that refresh your spirit, broaden your horizons, and leave you with stories to tell for years.

Just The Essential Disney Hacks: Discounts & Fun From Booking To Visit

This is the ultimate guide for enjoying Disney World on a budget. This book is packed with insider tips, money-saving strategies, and practical advice to help you get the most out of your Disney experience without overspending. Whether you're a first-time visitor or a seasoned Disney fan, you'll discover ways to make your trip magical and affordable.

www.ingramcontent.com/pod-product-compliance
Lightning Source LLC
Chambersburg PA
CBHW052146220526
45471CB00004B/1548